AMERICA'S WALLS

AMERICA'S WALLS

Tom Forbes

iUniverse, Inc.
Bloomington

America's Walls

iUniverse books may be ordered through booksellers or by contacting:

iUniverse
1663 Liberty Drive
Bloomington, IN 47403
www.iuniverse.com
1-800-Authors (1-800-288-4677)

ISBN: 978-1-4620-7373-3 (sc)
ISBN: 978-1-4620-7374-0 (hc)
ISBN: 978-1-4620-7375-7 (e)

Library of Congress Control Number: 2011962707

Printed in the United States of America

iUniverse rev. date: 01/09/2012

Author's Personal Disclosure

If I have misquoted or provided incorrect statistics or facts in my book, I apologize to any and all who may be offended by the errors. I will tell you this up front because I don't want any of you to be misled into thinking I misstated or shared unfounded facts in an effort to prepare myself for a future in politics.

Contents

Preface

The contents of this book discuss several events and problems the American people and their government face today. Each chapter represents a specific problem as viewed through the concerned eyes of just one man (who is average in education, average in dreams, a tad more then average in income, and maybe a bit above average in love of his country). The contents of this book were not put together to deface the workings of the United States government or to insult its executive branch or, for that matter, to insult any part of our government.

On the contrary, I as the author care with all my heart about this nation, its president, and all those who claim the title of American. I served this nation for nearly twenty-five years as a US Marine. However, I write not as a former Marine; I write as an angry American citizen who is tired of a government that turns a deaf ear to the voice of the people. Yes, turns a deaf ear to those who make up the working class of this land—its majority people, its working middle-class population.

Each chapter of this book discusses issues that concern average working-class people across the nation, and as its author, I believe the thoughts and ideas within each chapter represent the feelings and mind-set of the majority of the American people.

Middle-class America—this unheard voice, this silent majority—is not and has not been heard or represented in government lately. This I *strongly* believe. My fellow forgotten friends, this must change. As this book's author, I can tell you I am no Mr. Smith who goes to Washington, but I would support any candidate who resembled that man.

It is my hope that you readers will rally around much of this book's contents and begin to speak out to anyone who will listen. I also hope you will help me prove that one person's voice can make a difference and that, united, our voices can awaken America and bring back its values, traditions, and dollar. Let our voices be the catalysts for reform and good things to come for the America we love.

Our government is too fat; it's unhealthy, just as any obese human would be if he had grown to the brink of bodily destruction. We need to shrink it for its own health and well-being, and for ours too.

We the people of this nation are not stupid, and we are not dumb, but we do seem to be voiceless. Or are we just being ignored? We must not only be heard, but our thoughts must be answered by our government leaders. And if that thought doesn't sit well with them, then maybe they need to find another seat.

The American Knucklehead Hats and T-Shirts are available for purchase by following the ordering information found at the end of the book.

Acknowledgments

I would like to extend a special thanks to my family for the encouragement they gave me in completing this book. Thanks also to my friend Betty Usher for her help and encouragement along the way.

And special thanks to Martin Mercy, my pal, for not only encouraging this book but also for all the conversations that took place between us that very much helped construct the thoughts for many of its pages and chapters. Excuse me, but it was more like the hours we spent talking shit about Harry Reed and wondering how the hell he got reelected.

Introduction

During the Lincoln-Douglas debates of 1858, Abraham Lincoln made the statement that he disagreed with the following practice: "You work and toil and earn bread, and I will eat it." Of course in that day, he was talking about the evils of slavery. Today he might say exactly those same words, but he would likely mean the 51 percent of the nation's citizens who toil, work, and earn bread while the other 49 percent eat it.

Americans are pissed off, and why shouldn't they be? In particular, it is the middle-class working Americans who are angry. Remember them? They are the people of this land who go to work day after day and work hard to catch a piece of the American dream—a dream that seems more difficult to grasp every day as the government expands its role in our people's day-to-day freedoms.

The people who make up the American middle class are taxed hard, *excessively hard*, and as they stand by and watch, the value of dollars they earn spirals downward. Imagine, the American dollar today is worth about twelve cents on the world market. But fear not, the Obama administration is solving the problem with lessons obtained from the Moe, Larry, and Curly Institute of Economic Growth and Money Management. Yes, our government is solving the problem of America's weak currency by—*you guessed it*—printing barrels of new money.

Yes, the Obama administration has printed more dollars in its first-term tenure than all past administrations in the history of our nation put together. The latest round of this madness has increased our money supply by almost 300 percent. Why didn't I think to do that? I didn't think of it because it is a ridiculous step to take to solve America's financial problems, not to mention just a stupid thing to do. If they keep it up, soon it will cost twenty dollars for a loaf of bread. I didn't think of printing more money because I am just one of the millions of brainless Americans whose unheard voice happens to represent most of the population of this country (middle-class America to be exact).

What is going on in America? The fact is that we are a nation founded on values, many of which are slowly and steadily being removed from the American lifestyle. And our government is accepting these changes and seems to be acting on behalf of those who want to change it. It's time we speak out against such foolishness. My friends, we are not brainless, but we *are* voices that are not being heard. My God, American children are on the verge of losing the right to recite the pledge of allegiance to our flag as we know it, and they may be losing the right to say it altogether. No more "one nation under God." And what has happened to God in America? No longer is prayer acceptable in schools or workplaces. Oh, I forgot. I'm not supposed to say *God. How ridiculous!* And we now even have US congressmen who question and show lack of concern for the writings within the United States Constitution.

As a former Marine and a proud American, I have to ask, what the hell is going on? I say to all who will listen, we must keep an eye on America's walls. We must protect the fabric of America's walls and their foundation, that foundation being our Constitution, our values, our heritage, our freedom, and our liberty as defined by our forefathers. And most of all, we must protect and demand that the people's voices be heard by our government, not with a deaf ear but with a response and the passion to serve.

America's middle class citizens are suffering as they continue to slide down the economic ladder. Why? The average American believes the answer to this question stems from our nation's leaders' lack of true insight and response to the real issues of the day. Our nation's leaders continuously avoid the real problems that plague our country because the real problems, in a word, are too hard and too challenging for them to tackle.

Do you blame them for avoiding the difficult issues? After all, it would be dangerous to them as individual statespersons to take a firm and decisive stance on a controversial issue. *Yes, I blame them.* Failure to seek answers to the difficult issues is the reason why our nation is in the midst of some of these god-awful problems.

Day after day, American leadership continues to exacerbate the truly difficult problems by tossing the blame for them from party to party; it's as if they are playing a game of hot potato. Stop blaming each other, stop tossing the potato around, and solve the damn problems. By the way, unlike our nation's politicians, I don't talk pretty and I'm not pretty, but I will fight. Hey American leadership, we the American people are tired of the political dancing. We don't like the games you play, and our liking of you is becoming more and more questionable. Don't you realize that avoiding the real issues is like failing to respond to a serious illness? We are tired of seeing you covering up and hiding America's cancerous areas with cheap talk and small Band-Aids that serve no real purpose. Americans elected you so you would target the *real* problems.

Leaders of America's people, we ask that you to be not political salespeople but instead that you be leaders. Be recognized as statespeople, and most importantly, be leaders with unwavering American ideals that enter into every decision you make. Come out of your corners and *fight*, you pantywaist sissies.

I can't believe that as an American citizen I listened to the 2007 presidential debates and heard a mix of celebrated candidates speak long on the topic of driver's licenses for illegal immigrants. Why didn't all of you stand up and say, "The question is ridiculous. I won't discuss it. I will not respond to the question because the problem's root is illegal immigration, not drivers' licenses. The problem to solve is protecting our borders from those who would cross it illegally. Now if you want to talk about that, then I will give you an answer."

Damn it, if only one of you in the room had had the nuts to say that. A couple of you came close, but no one came through, and that is the story of America's politics lately: avoid the real issues.

Chapter 1:

Illegal Immigration

Illegal Mexican immigrants babies born in the United States—every one of these cute little bubbly beauties is to be called an American, with all rights that come along with it. So says the American government. Who out there could have a problem with that happening? Well, the government of Mexico for one. It is my understanding that Mexican law doesn't disown these babies as citizens of their land as result of birth outside their nation (when both birth parents are citizens of Mexico).

The American Constitution in this case opens a door that contributes to population growth, not just the child born into our Nation, but as well lining up the illegal immigrant parents for other forms of U S Government dependency all through the side door of the babies birth. Side doors of all kinds are destroying our Nation and in all contributing to the bankrupting of America by allowing this. Perhaps law relating could be amended to look after the American citizens, in particular the ones that pay taxes and work every day of their lives. Some Americans label these babies as tickets or family glue to American citizenship; whatever we Americans call them, they are really tiny beautiful citizens of a neighboring country, perhaps amendment need be in place to reflect that thought. The parent(s) of said babies perhaps should be Americans by law prior to the babies birth before the childs citenzenship is stamped U S. When are we going to figure out that America gains nothing from those who enter our country illegally? Yes, we at times get enthusiastic, good workers who can be hired cheap and who are willing to do most anything for the dollars paid. However, the US government receives no tax revenue from these workers, and every job gained by these illegal hands is a job lost by an American.

On top of all that, the US economy says bye-bye to much of the wages earned by these non-American hands, as many of these people funnel the money they have earned right back across the border, never to be used for the growth of America's economy. American dollar after American dollar is now providing shelter and food for Mexican people while at the same time bolstering Mexico's economy. What's wrong with this picture?

What about the individual US states where these non-Americans work and reside? How are they making out as result of this foreign gain? Well, California would tell you that in a period of a year this particular population of people cost it tax dollars to a tune of nearly twenty billion dollars, all hard-earned dollars sacrificed by California taxpayers and all directed to the *care and chaos* relating to the welfare of these illegal American freedom seekers. Someone needs to advise the California governor that the money saved at the end of a year would be near the money required to heal the preponderance California deficit if the illegal immigration problem in this country was addressed.

Welfare is the most abused and misused word in the English language. Note: Mexicans are not the only border crossers that fall into the category of illegal immigrants entering our country;

however, they as a group represent around 90 percent of the illegal population present in America today.

America is the melting pot of all different people, races, and religions, and that fact is honestly where our nation gathers its true beauty. But if you desire to come join us from any country around the world, we ask that you please use the front door—the door associated with proper immigration into our nation—because we are tired of those who would illegally enter our home. Can we not get this point across to the leadership of this great nation? Obviously not.

Think about it. Is entering the United States illegally any different than an intruder entering your family's home? If you answer the question honestly, you would answer with a resounding *no*.

America has never in its past history needed to protect its borders from illegal crossing as the America of the today must do or learn to do. If we have to realign the armed forces to do so, then let it be. Think about it, protecting our borders would be an army in a defensive posture, protecting and defending its perimeter. Does that sound familiar, soldiers, airman, Marines, and sailors? It sounds like Defensive Soldering 101 to me.

As I look back, I remember a presidential candidate who stood boldly in front of his fellow candidates during a debate and made the statement that the United States Armed Forces were not designed to safeguard/guard our nation's borders. After serving in the Marines for twenty-five years, I would have liked to have said to that idiot, "What the hell do you think we have been doing in every war scenario we have been involved in for the past two decades?" Oh, you're right. We weren't protecting our borders; we were protecting borders all over the world and doing so at the expense of America's armed forces and the lives of America's youth.

We are so screwed up at this point when it comes to illegal immigrants overtaking our borders, homeland, and livelihoods that our American televisions are speaking Spanish to them now; Spanish-speaking commercials are airing in every state in America. Did we forget Americans speak English? My God, have you no respect for our heritage? We have already lost respect for our God by not putting up resistance to the asinine views of the ungodly and foreign influence. Is now our language to fall next in this illegal immigration business?

I as an American citizen should not have to learn to speak Spanish to be entertained by the television in my living room or in any other place within the United States. No, if you want to be an American, learn to speak English. I say to the following to those and only those who enter this nation properly: if you want to speak Spanish, French, Vietnamese, Greek, etc., then let that language you carried into America now be your second language because here in America, we speak English, as did the founders of the nation itself.

In closing, our nation's leaders have recently abandoned past immigration laws by authorizing any and all illegal immigrants to stay in America. That's right, they can't be deported unless a criminal past enters into the picture. American people, if you think you had it difficult getting a job at a decent wage in the recent past, get ready because as result of this act has, your ability to get hired, wages, and the chances of finding a hire have been reduced. Some of you think all immigrants do in this country is pick vegetables. Stand by. You're about to learn how wrong you are. Keep an eye on how employment in America changes. The job market will be flooded with illegal immigrants (flooded in all occupations, with no boundaries). Why? Because contractors, for example, can now legally hire from this massive illegal manpower source and pay them jack-shit wages in comparison to what they paid you.

There will be no boundaries and no job limits anymore: dry wall finisher, dozer operators, electricians, factory line workers, carpenters, doctors, and—God forbid—more attorneys, etc. Now, I always try to look to the positive end, and the positive I see in all these new immigrant attorneys is that at least these attorneys work for minimum wage.

Are you worried about the walls yet? Not yet? Well, keep reading.

Chapter 2:

The War on Terrorism

To me, the war on terrorism had legs immediately after the destructive September 11 terrorist attack. However, looking back at our response and the lives that were lost responding to the scene, combined with the billions of dollars spent fighting this so-called war, I would compare the overall US operation in the Arab world to a man getting rid of a mosquito in his home by setting his house on fire and accidentally burning it down in the process. In my eyes, the bottom line is there is no logic to what we are doing in the Arab nations in 2011–2012, and there will be none in the future.

We are not war fighting. Do we not know, have we not learned that an American GI walking the streets of these Arab nations dressed in his or her American desert camouflage war gear is nothing more than a target of opportunity for the bad guys? Dear God, have we forgotten the principles of war fighting *again*?

We lost them someplace in Vietnam, found them later in the first Gulf War, and have lost them again in Iraq, Afghanistan, etc. The principles of war say things like "gain and maintain contact with the enemy" and "keep the enemy tired, off guard, and constantly moving while destroying him and his will to fight." The only will to fight I see dwindling is ours. Even the village idiot can see we are not following any portion of any such war-fighting principles.

However, if we decide to go over there to destroy the place and take the land and oil, I'll be happy to go. That would be real war fighting, with a clear objective assigned. I'm old, but I'd like to go on that ride.

Can't we see that because there are no clear objectives in this war and no clear enemy in sight, it's just not an *army* war; it's a special ops war, possibly a political war, and sadly, political wars just end up killing our country's youth for no goddamn good reason at all. I don't care how many books George Bush writes (and I love and respect him). After the SEAL team killed that knucklehead Osama bin Laden, at this point if a reason exists to keep it going, it is so secretive and perhaps foul that the American people aren't supposed to know what it is.

While campaigning, President Obama said he would end the involvement and bring our servicemen and women home. Maybe he will make the move just prior to the 2012 election. What do you think? Let's face it. The only good thing that comes out of these Arab nations is oil, and if I had my guess about the secret to the war, it would be *oil related.*

The fact is that this type of war fighting, if you can call it war fighting, could go on forever and end up costing a lot GIs their lives. If the Obama administration supports this so-called war, they need to take a few hours and talk it over in the desert, dressed in the uniform of a GI, strolling down the dangerous and deadly streets our military people traverse daily. They will never comprehend the madness and terror of the situation until they feel the heat and see the killing firsthand.

It is easy to make life and death decisions when your life is not one of those in danger. The only real danger to our government leadership is in when it comes to this war is the remote possibility that someone could drop a dead American's casket on one of their feet while they sit in attendance at a burial service. It is also easy to support a war when you don't really know what war is. Heck, the Vietnam War would have been over much sooner had the Paris peace talks been held in Vietnam in a fighting hole at the foot of the Rockpile.

American fighting men and woman are the very soul of this nation. They are men and women who walk into danger for our country's well-being. (P.S., I really enjoyed former President Bush's book. I think he's a good guy.) I think all American presidents are good guys. I just pray I'm right. Oh, I forgot. I am not supposed to say a prayer. Bullshit, it's my book, so I'll do it anyway.

The American GIs never falter; they stow their fears and bravely and honorably defend our nation. Many of us Americans may question this war fight we're in, but never do we slight the heroes that fight and die in actions associated with the operation and its not-so-clear intent. These brave men and women honor us, our flag, our history, and everyone who wore the uniforms before them. The Iraq and Afghanistan veterans will go down in history as some of the bravest of all. God Bless the US Armed Forces. (By the way, three cheers for the SEALs for killing that bastard Osama bin Laden). Our military, my friends, is the strongest part of our nation's walls; they guard and protect this country. Never forget that. We need not let them be abused.

One thing is for sure: if we had elements of our armed forces on the job of protecting our borders, we wouldn't be worrying about illegal immigrants with driver's license issues. (P.S., sometimes I don't speak very nicely, but don't judge me. Remember Matthew 7:1.)

Chapter 3:

Military Cutbacks

The US same government that won't take our GIs out of the dangers associated with the current desert war now intends to cut back capabilities of the US Armed Forces. Who the hell is the genius behind this kind of thinking? You can bet he is not a current GI. Surely it's not our president, but I think I might smell Harry Reed. And surely John McCain didn't sign off on that.

In 2011 and 2012, our country's government is planning military cutbacks, everything from reducing the size of our military to cutting back on ship building and the research and development of weapons systems, etc. Yes, less beans, bullets, and Band-Aids, but they are still willing to send your ass to war. How's that sound, America?

If that sounds good to you, don't forget to send in for your American Knucklehead Hat. And friends, if you know a knucklehead who may warrant the wearing of such a hat, feel free to pick one up for him or her.

America has got to be on the cutting edge in our ability to war fight. When I say war fight, I don't mean this shit we are currently doing. My God, it is 2011 and it seems every third-world nation is developing weapon systems that can produce mass destruction. At the same time, boldly in front of all onlookers, they are building armies and navies, and what is America's response? Missile treaties with Russia and cutbacks to our military.

You might be saying, well a missile treaty with a formative foe seems like an extremely wise path to follow under the current world conditions. Maybe so, if the treaties didn't lead to lesser capability of the United States in the end.

And as I understand, we agreed to a new nuclear treaty with Russia that lets others influence how we grow and what and when we are to dismantle. Who in the hell was the brains behind that one? How do you feel about the walls now, America?

If I have given you mixed emotions about the use of our armed forces, allow me to straighten that out for you right now. Our nation's armed forces must be well prepared, well trained, and well armed in order to meet and, more importantly, exceed any other world power. At the same time, I don't believe we need to be engaged in crises that do not pertain to the welfare or safety of our nation and its people. I, like most other Americans, do not desire our nation's armed forces to be the international police and or security force for nations around the globe. We have to get out of that business now and stay out of it forever.

Our United States, its people, and its borders must be protected at all costs. The very best way we can protect all of that is to be as Ronald Reagan suggested: the strongest kid on the block. And all contenders must consider us as just that. We cannot have leadership that is satisfied with our country being a second-rate power in any way—militarily, economically, scientifically, etc.

With the above thought in mind, reducing the effectiveness of today's armed forces is not the answer; cutbacks to our military must not be on the table at a time in history, especially when so much military growth is visible around the world. In particular, it should not be on the table when that growth represents a threat to our nation. If we must cut down on this nation's wasteful spending, let the cuts begin in the midst of this country's most insane spending wasteland: you guessed it, unearned entitlement programs (to be continued in a later chapter).

All this being said, we really can reduce spending in the armed forces without restricting its effectiveness, and we can do so—wisely, I might add—by closing down some or many overseas US bases that no longer have significant applications to today's military strategies. Bases such as these *do* support nations, just not ours. In 2011 and 2012, the United States has the means to fast and effectively support large-scale deployment to any sector of the globe, all from pretty much right here in the United States.

Now, I'm not saying close *all* the overseas bases; some likely have some strategic worth left. But I am saying we should remove the ones that don't have any purpose, and then we should continue to develop procedures and tactics to support deployment from limited geographical sectors. We need to focus our resources on creating a designed action that will be capable of meeting any threat anywhere in the world.

Another good reason for cutting back on overseas bases is the fact that our nation has nuclear submarines that can deploy tremendous destruction in any place at any time, God forbid. (Oh, I forgot I am not supposed to say God these days. Well, too bad again. This is *my* book, and I will say it if I want to.) These atomic vessels and ships continuously cruise the depths of oceans all over globe, locations unknown anyone outside the need to know. Should problems abroad need be stifled, this threat alone is a real keep-you-in-check maker. One sub is worth ten-plus overseas military installations.

Remember as well that these overseas bases do more supporting of the economies of the countries in which they are located than supporting real-world missions in the 2011 and 2012. God knows America does not need to support other countries with our military bases. Closing many of these bases would allow tremendous savings in military budget; such removal could shift billions into military defense and at the same time provide the necessary funds to start protecting our borders. Think about it.

We Americans are blessed with a powerful navy that can fight, carry, and convoy troops around the globe; we can't afford to cut back on ship building. Cuts in ship building budgets in this day and age are absolutely crazy, especially for certain types of ships. Now more than ever in our history we must depend on the navy to move men and equipment, not to mention that we need the ships to war fight. And don't forget nuclear submarines (the best deterrent going).

I would like to end this chapter with the following thought: if a GI is to die, let his or her death be marked in the pages of service to his or her country, not highlighted by service relating to any other nation. For God's sake, is anyone listening? Our military must serve the purpose of protecting America, its lands, and its people. It must not serve nations of far-off lands, protecting substances like Arab oil, and if you don't believe that is happening, someone needs to send you a American Knucklehead Hat right away.

Our armed forces are supposed to protect our way of life. Our people are to be used for the welfare of US citizens. Our government needs to start concerning itself with that thought, wouldn't you say? *Welfare*—the most abused misused word in the English language. I will expound on that word in future chapters.

So what do you think of America's walls now? Strong, weak, barely holding? What do you think?

Chapter 4:

Alternative Fuels and Travel

How many of you out there believe all Arabs make their living off of selling Americans oil at outrageous prices? Not many of you, I'm sure, realize it's the wealthy Arab leaders that see most of that money, not the Arab people.

Americans think of the Arab world with visions of oil rich sheiks, oil wells, and the radical Muslim Brotherhood, which as a whole hates the American people. We think of people that burn our flags and beat and rape news girls in the street while only the women of the country come to her aid. Truly, the people of the Arab nations do not hate Americans; most of them just can't stand our government and our way of life, religion, and people. And that's about it.

Oh heck, none of that is true. Maybe they love us. But I ask you, what is strange about nations who could hate Americans holding us hostage with oil prices? Answer: not a thing. These Arab nations will control oil prices, and as long as they are the big suppliers, it's simple Arab economics: we go to them, and they charge the shit out of us infidels.

We mean little to them; we are godless creatures to them. When I was in the Gulf War, these people expected us to move to the other side of the sidewalks as they walked by in their spotless white gowns. Bullshit. That wasn't going to happen, not with the Marines. Yeah, they look down on us, but they will take us for every dime they can and spill our blood in battle to protect themselves and their stinking oil. Americans, we are just a bunch of godless infidels. You didn't know that?

In my eyes, oil is always the bottom line when it comes to America sticking its nose in the problems of the day in these Arab countries. I feel it's been that way since Desert Storm and every intervention since. (Sorry, every *war* since.) Have you not felt that way? Sure you have. Oil today is used in everything from making plastics to heating homes. This entire country revolves around the use of oil in one way or another. And because of that, when we speak of research to get out of the oil business, we must think of more than one alternative fuel source. Our research must extend in all directions, not just in fuels for home heating or road travel. We need to find fuel for all things, fuel that comes from as many sources as possible. The word *many* is most important to our future. We cannot afford to put all our eggs in one basket ever again. It seems like our government keeps refusing to seek fuel sources from within our own nation.

My God, there is more coal in Wyoming than in any place in the world. Coal as a lone source of energy would keep our furnaces going for five hundred years, and that's just from Wyoming alone, but environmentalist are on the way to curbing the use of this natural resource. Leave it to the tree-hugger shit stirrers. We always overreact, always go to extremes, and always hurt our nation when we do so.

I served in the Gulf War and breathed oil-filled air for months as that former idiot Saddaam Hussien and his army torched hundreds upon hundreds of oil wells. With our nation's stiff control over our coal industry, in a million years we couldn't hurt the environment with our use of coal any more than those stupid bastards did in that one episode of lunacy. Get real, America. Find oil in our land and off our coastal areas, find and mine our coal, build wind turbines, and seek out any other energy source available to relieve us of our dependence on Arab oil.

Let's talk about travel fuel in relationship to automobiles. First remember that Americans shouldn't have to pay as much for a car as we do for the homes we live in. That sentence is for you SOBs that build cars.

I hear these electric cars can travel in excess of three hundred miles per charging. I'm thinking out loud now: Let's see, the average American drives less than thirty miles per day. With that thought in mind, this estimate is aimed at approximately 90 percent of the US driving population.

Well heck, to me that sounds like we have a pretty good reason to wean ourselves off the desert bandits' oil reserves. And at the same time, we have at least one start on the alternative fuel chart available. But remember, we cannot stop with electric sources alone. Automobiles (land rollers) must be propelled by multiple sources if we are truly to escape the clutches of the oil bandits of the world who would hold us hostage and love to see our nation in chaos.

We need reach deep in our research bags and seek out many new fuel sources. Let's get busy, America, and get the United States's automobiles, busses, trains, and even airplanes powered by energy sources other than imported oil. If anyone is to hold United States economy in their hands, it should that of the people of United States, not the world of the Arab brothers. I could never be president; I'd go over there, kick their asses, and take the oil. (Just kidding, I think.)

Look at the trains of today and how they have reduced the use of oil (fuel). The technology is out there. However, like my old football couch used to say, "You got to want it. You *really* got to want it."

We must understand that lowering the need for oil in turn lowers requirement for its use, and that's really the issue of the day. However, I don't believe any 2007-2008 or 2011-2012 presidential candidates from either political party could truly outline such a plan. Do you think 2012 will be any different? The current administration has not proven that the subject of refueling is of much importance as an agenda item. We spend more time kissing the new Arab regimes as each new uprising triggers a new government under new leadership.

Remember this: currently more than 70 percent of the United States's oil needs are dependent on imported oil. Now, that's not to say we don't have untapped oil reserves of our own, because we do. Let's talk about our own country's oil. Start by asking yourself why China would be able search for oil off the California coast but we can't. To me that's bullshit. Are we worried about accidents (e.g., oil spills) off the coast? Well, I'd be more worried about a country that can't sell toothpaste outside its own country because of health dangers drilling for oil off the coast of my nation. If China can't control its toothpaste manufacturers, what makes you think they are going to safely drill oil off this country's shores, or for that matter, any shore that does not belong to them? I guess you've got to give them something when you continue to borrow money from them.

Do you think our government knew back in the early 70s that our oil supply was predicted to be at inadequate levels to meet our nation's need today? Sure they did. And *now* the question is what did they do correct the situation? *Nothing* is the answer. And every administration thereafter has followed suit. The question now is what will today's American leaders do? Past leadership went outside our borders, and as result we became dependent on other nations to supply us with oil. Why the hell did we not search within our own borders? And let me ask you this, will we buy oil that has been drilled off California's coast from China? Think about it. I feel the answer is surely that we will …

Friends, this is all simple economics that is now teaching us a lesson and kicking our ass at the same time. It's simple supply and demand: they got it, we need it, and they charge the shit out of us in the buying process. As a result, our entire American economic structure has been affected by extreme prices attached to anything and everything associated with fuel. This fuel issue has caused changes in everything from food prices to whether or not we visit our grandparents this year. Had we moved on the problem in the 50s and 60s, our dependence on Arab oil wouldn't exist today.

Yet here we are today, in the midst of Arab conflict. We provide Arab nations safety at the cost of American taxpayers and at the same time put American lives at risk, and we are doing so not to protect a true ally but instead to protect a nation of people who can't stand us. (This of course is my opinion.) Will they be required to foot any of the bills for the help provided? Hell no. What will the United States gain? Only higher prices at the pumps. In the long run we might even provide the rebels with weapons of war. I can see this happing. I can also see them using those weapons against American GIs in the future. When will the madness end?

We respond not in a kick-ass battle of applied research and development, seeking ways to wean ourselves off Arab oil, but instead we try to make these people who I believe hate us somehow like us. It is not going to happen. And once again, when the smoke clears, they will use more high-priced Arab oil to keep a firm grip on America's economy. They will use that resource, and they will continue to hurt us. Does anyone not believe that? We had better find oil on our own property and/or alternative fuel sources. There are lots of folks much smarter than I who say America has plenty of oil that we are just not going after. *Why?* Instead we do not act. We do nothing. Why? Because our government does not—as stated on the first page of this book—like to go after the real and the hard issues. (Hell, with the party war going on in House and Senate, our leaders can't agree on anything these days.)

Heck, we could give shovels to all the lazy entitlement-grabbing bastards that live off the government and assign them to start digging. There are enough of them that they could dig through the earth to a point where we could retrieve oil from the other side of the globe. Heck, we could take the Arab oil without them being the wiser. (Just kidding, I think.)

Well then, should we blame the government? Damn right we should. Who else? Our government leadership is to blame. You know, in the Marines we had an expression; we'd say, well it's pretty, but can it *fight*? I think we should ask this same question of any person we chose to elect to public office. Instead of pretty faces, cute smiles, and fast talk, we need to ask if the SOB can fight and, more importantly, if he or she will fight for the people of this land. Stop bullshitting around, and *start looking for fuel!*

Chapter 5:

Stimulus

timulus—a fun word turned to shit with just a couple applications by the American government. Hell, if the United States government is going to give billions upon billions of taxpayer dollars to banks and to the auto industry, wouldn't you think they would have demanded follow-up regarding the use of those dollars? Wouldn't you have expected them to demand that those companies show that those dollars were spent wisely and constructively?

If I go to a bank for money, you can be sure they are going to want an explanation of how and what I will use the money for. What if I was a company CEO requesting the money and in the process I told the bank I intended to use large portions of the loan to give my business executives million-dollar bonuses? Well surely the bank's answer would surely have been, "Are you freaking kidding me? Hell no, we are not giving you the loan."

The government should have insisted that those companies put forth a plan. They should have are protected our taxpayer dollars. What has the American taxpayer gained with all the government stimulus? I will tell you what we have gained: higher taxes down the road and higher-priced automobiles

This to me would have been a great time to say, "Banks and auto industries, we will give you this money; however, portions of it must be used for research and development of transportation powered by alternative fuel for America."

The government of the United States of America gave out massive amounts of tax dollars without any idea how the money was going to be used by these entities. I'd rather see my taxes burnt in the basement of the IRS than have billions handed out in form of government stimulus with no rules for use or the means to follow up on the handling or management of those funds. I don't think anyone in government has any idea how or what this money was used for. Does this sound reckless to anyone else? An even better—and maybe more important—question would be, what happen to the dollars reported paid back by some of the entities?

Anybody know how I might get a stimulus loan? I can tell you what I would use it for. I'd pay taxes with it.

Chapter 6:

What Happened to America's Jobs?

Who is to blame? You are, American workers. Take some of credit for the American job loss, and place the blame squarely on your own dumb asses, you greedy bastards. That's right, you need to take some of the blame for these jobs disappearing and being outsourced all over the globe. China is paying their auto workers ten cents an hour to build US automobiles. I ask you, how do you compete with that? You *don't*. Remember those unions you started and couldn't live without? Remember all they did for you in the beginning? They helped you acquire good pay, health benefits, etc. What the hell what happened? What happened was greed drank the well dry and didn't blink until the jobs were gone.

Damn it, boys and girls. Did you not realize bringing home the same salary as the vice president of the United States was part of your doom as an assembly-line worker in your neighborhood Chrysler plant? As a union worker, did you ever ask yourself what part union leadership played in the money disappearing and jobs alongside it? You union workers should ask yourselves that question if you haven't already. It's not all unions; I know that, as do you. There is great good in unions, providing that they hold themselves to their original purpose of providing goods for the workers.

However, beware of the nasty little one-syllable word that often accompanies union operations: *greed*. And let's not forget the greed of the manufacturers and how it plays into the picture. Face it, boys and girls: if the car manufactures can get the job done at two-tenths the cost by building the product in Mexico (for example), then why not? Hell, our own government opens the doors (thank you, Bill). And it's not just the auto industries; all kinds of American industries use product builders outside the country today, and all for very much the same reason: they can get it done cheaper. More profit on the sales side combines nicely with less money invested on the building side. It all makes sense.

Made in America, now that's a statement that just doesn't make the noise it use to. It doesn't bring in the money, unless you're making babies in an effort to fatten your welfare check. If you don't think the statement *Made in America* has lost its original zeal, just ask any dollar bill. And that, my average American friend, must change. This kind of talk must reverse and never come again. American industry, building, and manufacturing must once again be surrounded by words like *quality* and *pride* and supplied by the will and power of the people of the United States.

People must learn to be supported by a reasonable income. For the life of me, I can't see why it's not on every presidential candidate's list for hopeful accomplishments. That thought must be driven in to the mind-set of all Americans. Bring the jobs back to America, and Americans have to work at a salary reasonable for the work they are performing. This idea alone, more than anything else, will change the world of economic growth for the better in this country. Thoughts pertaining to the above idea are the kind of topics presidential debates should focus on instead of questions about illegal immigrants' driver's licenses. I wonder how many hours candidates put into preparing answers for the driver's license question.

What do you think about America's walls now?

Chapter 7:

Unemployment Insurance

I t's a bad idea when the process is abused. And boy is it ever abused. By the way, our government leadership is absolutely leading the abuse in this particular subject. Why? Because the vote that continues to extend this handout is politically driven. We will speak more on the subject of politically driven issues later.

The problem with unemployment dollars is that while the unemployment checks are rolling in like clockwork, nonworking Americans don't pay much attention to the clock. Unemployed people's job searches are driven by two variables, and the United States government is oblivious to both of them. The first variable is if I am unemployed and I have several months of unemployment wages to count on in the upcoming calendar year, I am not going to look for just any job, particularly if it doesn't meet my expectations for what I think I am worth in the job market.

As matter of fact, when the checks first start dancing in, I may not look at for anything for a while. Yes, I will make a couple phone calls so I can check off the monthly effort-made box to cover my ass. Hey, I deserve a little time off and this unemployment entitlement can keep up with the basics, for a while anyway. Hell, it's an entitlement. I rate it as an American citizen. After all, isn't that what entitled means? (If you don't believe this attitude exists, tell me the address where your friends need to send your American Knucklehead Hat.)

The second variable our government has failed to recognize is that the unemployed most likely will not seriously look hard at employment opportunities until they feel the government handout is near an end. At that point, they are hungry for employment and will not only concede to a less-than-ideal job, but they will happily take almost anything. Because at that point, the old hierarchy of needs comes into play. They might say to themselves, "If I don't take this job, I may find myself without a pot to piss in or a widow to throw it out of in the near future. Not to mention my family may starve if I keep being stupid in this job-hunting ordeal."

I bet there is not a man or women in this nation who does not know at least one person, heck more like two or three, who is currently or has in the past milked the shit out of unemployment income. To add insult to injury, instead of putting a stop to it, our knucklehead leadership instead plays politics with the subject and extends, extends, and extends unemployment benefits once again.

They haven't figured out that we hard-working, taxpaying Americans don't want to know how kind and gentle spirited these men and women who lead our country are. No, we want to see them respond to difficult decisions. Damn it, we expect intelligent decisions, not decisions based on how good it makes them look to the weak-minded of our nation. If this country wants to put people to work, all it has to do is stop rewarding the unemployed over and over again. Yes, give them a shot at unemployment income, but put an end to it as well. End the handout, and in turn make them responsible for their lives again.

The fact is that the failure to remove the handout is the exact problem that festers within all unearned entitlements. People will take part in them, draw from them, and live off of them for as long as the system allows them to, for as long as that relief handout is intended. Why not? It's free to them. However, it is very costly to working America's tax base.

The scary part about the handout entitlement is that in time the recipients forget how and why it was given in the first place, and all of a sudden it becomes more than a temporary helping hand; it becomes a lifetime survival mechanism. I would bet if we put a stop to these continuous extensions on various entitlement activities, America's unemployment statistics would take very quick turn for the better. People will get jobs. I spent some time overseas as a Marine, and one thing I noticed was that the poor in foreign lands work. They work to survive and to take care of their loved ones. They forage for their food (in a word).

Now, President Obama speaks to his nation concerning a *jobs* plan. The plan is all about getting America back on its feet and its workers back on the job. Personally, I think what just happened with the illegal immigrants being given the authorized opportunity to stay in this country without fear of deportation has destroyed chances for many jobless Americans, not to mention any job plan aimed at getting Americans back to work. The action allowing any illegal immigrants to stay, my friends, cut American working men and women off at the knees. Why? Think about it: what contractor out to hire carpenters (for example) would select American workers when he or she had a tremendous pool of no-longer-illegal immigrants to choose from? Why pay hourly wages in the range of ten to thirty dollars an hour when they can now pull carpenters from the minimum-wage working corps? Jobs plan, my ass.

Chapter 8:

Public Housing

Is public housing a way out, or is it something else? Think with me for a moment: large groups of people who, for the most part, are not well educated, jobless, dependant on the government, of minority decent (in my particular part of the country anyway), and all living in the midst of properties and homes provided by the federal government. What does that spell out to you? In most cases, it spells no happy ending and no place else to go.

I ask you, has this government program changed lives for the better or helped people step up into new life pathways? Perhaps for some, but for the most part I believe it has confined people to the same communities that were built to initially help them. It started out as a good idea; however, when developing the program, the founders didn't have the insight to provide rules to control its use, at least not from the people perspective, and it wasn't for lack of trying but rather because of lack of recognition of what was to come.

Public housing should have rules limiting the duration of time a tenant can reside in government-funded housing. *Big error.* Temporary relief should have been on someone's mind when they laid out the rules, and because this did not take place, public housing throughout the nation has turned into multi-generational communities of people addicted to living off the US government and our taxes. Is there a way out for these people? Was the way out designed in the plan that established the housing movement? The answer is no. If so, show me. No, better yet, show and tell the people who reside in public housing how to escape it.

If the government took a real hard look, they would find that the preponderance of public housing dwellers are families who are social look-alikes. Many share one sorry day after another—each very much a reflection of the day before. Nothing changes. How do they escape? Think about it: large populations of people who are in many cases located in townships or areas that cannot support a large workforce and who are limited in range of employment skills and educational backgrounds. The bottom line is that in many communities there are only so many jobs available that don't require special skills and college educations, particularly in small communities. The problem comes when you insert an unskilled workforce whose population is ten times the available amount of unskilled labor jobs. What that means is simply that the other 90 percent of people desiring jobs will remain unemployed. It cannot and will not change. And that is a huge factor in the inability of people to leave public housing in many areas throughout our country. You might say that issue alone has erected the invisible bars that render them dependant on government assistance.

But how does one snap the chains of assisted government living once he or she has entered into it? Let's start by saying that many never do. And the ones that do, bless their hearts, have to be exceptional people—nonstop, never-give-up kind of folks. Sadly, many people never do, and frankly that question should have been asked and answered long before the government thought to go ahead with public housing, or for that matter with any unearned entitlement.

Without that question answered, public housing now becomes a breeding ground for much of America's poor population. It's not necessarily their fault; those invisible bars are hard to see. These same people, for the most part, are not only housed by the government, but they are also fed by the government. And for many, the energy/ utilities required to heat the house and cook the food is paid for by the government as well. Did I say paid for by the government? Wrong. You and I, working America, we pay every penny of it. And if you don't believe that, then frankly you need to put the book down and pick up the phone and order yourself you own personal American Knucklehead Hat.

Being addicted to public housing or any other unearned entitlement is plainly the result of being cared for at no expense of your own. *No work required.* People become accustomed to being taken care of. That thought, combined with not being aware of much of world outside, causes people to become lost in the world of government dependency.

Entitlements feed, clothe, and house many of these folks. They become lost and programmed, mentally convinced that this is what America offers them and that they are *entitled* to this free gift of never-ending dependency. The government gift of public housing started out as a temporary gift, I am sure of that. However, the word *temporary* never made it to print. The end result is that people have become strung out and addicted to the system.

It is very much like the story of the park bears. The story goes, people entering this particular national park allowed its visitors to feed the local bear community. This type feeding went on for years. They would feed the bears from their cars, with rangers standing by and actually overseeing the site. Years later, the park leadership decided that this behavior wasn't good for the bears and could be a danger to park visitors. So they enacted a new rule unauthorizing the feeding of the bears and instructed the park rangers to enforce it. With that, all patrons of the park stopped feeding the animals immediately.

However, what the park leadership had not reckoned was that the park bears had adjusted their eating behavior to being fed out of those friendly visitors' picnic baskets. As a result, the bears were stumped when the signs went up (even though they couldn't read them). The bears, as result of being hand-fed over the years, had lost something very important to their survival; they had lost their ability to forage for food on their own as nature intended them to. Their natural ability to survive, to fish and hunt meals for themselves, had been forgotten, and/or they had just become too lazy to want to revert to using those skills.

The younger bears, on the other hand, had never been taught to live off the land. They possessed little to no foraging skills. They'd been eating off the tourists since birth. (Thus we have generational addiction. Sound familiar?) The end result was that the visitors stopped feeding the bears as instructed by the park management, and the bears ... well, they began to attack park visitors and their belongings in an effort to feed themselves, just as some welfare check recipients attack the mail carriers when the welfare check doesn't hit the mailbox on the day they expect it. And if you think that doesn't happen, think again.

The bears had been fed by these people for years. Why stop now? Sounds a bit like today's welfare recipients and housing authority tenants. I once read that Mr. Roosevelt made the statement, "Welfare will become an addiction." Wasn't anyone listening?

I'm just a middle-class American, but I believe too much of anything at no cost makes a person care less for the value of what he or she has been given. If you don't believe these people are trapped, then think again.

To add insult to injury, our government's inept ability to recognize the root of problems now believes that cuts in operational funding for public housing is going to solve the problem. *Wrong again,* you knuckleheads. Cutting funds without reducing occupancy only makes it harder to keep the property safe, clean, and properly maintained. If you cut funds without reducing occupancy levels, you make slums and you make them dangerous places to live. You make it impossible for the directors, the caretakers, the managers, and the staff as a whole to care for properties and to properly and safely operate them.

Our United States government just doesn't get it. They need to take the following steps to solve the problem:

1. In order to reduce the funding to operate public housing units, the government must reduce the population of tenants and place restrictions on how long an individual can reside in them.
2. Those individuals cannot be allowed to return after the time restrictions end.
3. The numbers of properties should be reduced by very wisely removing the older and more costly to maintain properties. It can be done at the same time the population is being reduced as part of the time restriction now applied to tenant occupancy. This way, public housing on the average could be depleted by nearly a third of its population each year. (Sadly however, most of that same group will be back seeking reassignment within a short time. It's a vicious cycle, or should I say a vicious *recycle.* The government must stop that recycle in order to decrease the public housing population.)
4. Lastly, the government should drug test occupants. This alone will reduce tenant population drastically. (And don't

forget to make drug testing a mandatory requirement, with a minimum of two random screenings throughout the year, and always test with undisclosed dates and times.)

And don't give me any *we can't*. If you can drug test all the workers associated with public housing, then you can damn sure drug test the tenant population. And as a taxpaying American, I demand my tax dollars not be spent housing a population of drug users. So get on it! And don't tell me drug testing will cost too much. That coin has two sides: 1) the cost of drug testing and 2) the fact that once the testing is over, the public housing population will be decreased greatly and we would have made up the money for testing at that point.

Chapter 9:

The Entitlement Trap

rap sounds like a word too harsh to be applied to systems that were designed to reach out for such noble causes (e.g., welfare and care for America's poor and jobless, etc.). Today those programs mean so much more: for example, multiple free phones for drug dealers, among other things. Have you ever heard the expression "A good idea that stopped working"? Sure you have. Or was it a good idea that just didn't work? With those thoughts, I give you America—the land of entitlements.

When our forefathers spoke of the pursuit of happiness, I don't believe they were talking about living off of other people. Well, you say, how can we make demands of these poor, oppressed, jobless people (the same people, by the way, who in some cases are getting fatter by the hour). After all, they are just victims of a cruel world. If you believe that, you get no knucklehead hat; you are a just a plain idiot. Welfare programs of any kind have never been instrumental in curing problems in our nation. They plainly exacerbate them and just contribute to the plight in the long run.

Free rides should not last forever. And that is the biggest problem that leads to entitlement abuse. Any unearned entitlement should not last forever, and every entitlement should be worked for and paid for to the greatest degree possible by the individual drawing from it.

I can see folks drawing Social Security. Why not? Working men and women have funneled dollars in to that system for decades. I have since the age of seventeen, and like many of you, I deserve that income.

I guarantee you that if these handouts (the incomes provided by our tax dollars) had to be paid back or even if just portions of the money had to be returned, the programs would lose 85 percent of the users overnight, and back to work people would go. And our federal deficit would be on a fast road to recovery.

Most Americans would call today's welfare system a free ride. My God, we could cut that wasteful system back one-third by simply drug testing these poor victims of fate. Victims of fate? Bullshit. Instead, many of these people are victims of bad lifestyles, lifestyles that they have made for themselves. For the most part, they are victims of their own failure to educate themselves and take responsibility over their own lives. However, we dare not send that message to the National Welfare Rights Organization. Those people are out to reduce the eligibility standards for the programs again. They do not want reform; they are the reason the program has grown so incredibly large and has become so abusive to the taxpayers' dollars. This, of course, is my opinion. Yours too, huh? And it's a pretty good opinion at that.

This country's entitlement programs are very much out of control. The United States government makes it too easy to live off of it. I say make them earn it or pay it back (or some of it back), and most importantly, limit its use. What is so wrong with that concept? There is nothing wrong with it. Ask any hard-working American.

All cities have needs. For example, all cities have maintenance departments: road repair, and construction, maintenance work, park services, sanitation, administration. Cities also have public libraries, cafeterias, courthouses, etc.—all places public housing dwellers and welfare recipients could work productive hours in every day to pay for the gift of having a roof over their heads and food in their bellies.

Let no man ride free.

Some will tell you there is already a requirement in place for the housing authorities to enforce rules in this area. It came about as a law that I believe was called the Quality Housing and Work Responsibility Act. The problem is its mandatory hourly completion requirement is eight hours per month. Think about that: two hours a week. I guess they use the other thirty-eight working hours to beat the streets looking for employment. *Not.* I say there should be more of a requirement for the money to be paid back, more mandatory training, and more work assignments given to these folks. If someone lives off the government, then he or she has an obligation to that same government.

I believe it was President Kennedy that said, "Ask not what your country can do for you—ask what you can do for your country." What's wrong with President Kennedy's words in application to those who live off this nation? Nothing's wrong. His words are right on.

Handouts don't improve lives; they impair lives, and over the long term they literally destroy people's will to work. Are you trying to tell me our government has not figured that out?

How do you feel about the walls now?

Chapter 10:

Health Care

President Obama, bless his heart, went after a difficult one, a truly hard one. You have to give him credit for that. It is too bad that in doing so he sacrificed so many of his campaign promises. The promises about earmarks went out the door; I heard about six thousand of them were found in the health care bill alone. As for putting an end to deficit spending, I also hear that the health care bill will add $2.5 trillion to the deficit over the next few years.

Stop, damn it. The bill in its adopted state is the largest bill passed in the history of the United States. And it is the only one that was never read by the men and women who voted for it. I hope that somewhere in between those earmarks there are enough health care provisions to be helpful to the health needs of the American people and the nation it serves. I must say, I don't know enough about the bill to speak on its overall worth. I, like most Americans, just pray it doesn't ruin everything its pages of earmark extremes touch (e.g., future taxes, medical costs, insurance premiums, and the deficit). I guess we will find out those answers as the days pass.

The most disappointing thing about the passing of the health care bill is the fact that no House or Senate member read the bill prior to the vote. No, I am sorry. You can't tell me anyone one of them read it. Who the hell could read a bill the size of a New Jersey phone book, given the time constraints they had from the day they received it for review until the vote.

I want health care for all Americans. I love the President Obama as I love all presidents, but if I had to take a bet on whether or not he himself even read the entire thing, I would have bet against it. Both the Left and Right talk about the pros and cons relating to the bill, but in my opinion, none of them ever hit the mark—the mark being the process that allowed such a controversial bill to move forward and be approved in the first place.

This nation's health care bill is in place, yet no member of the Senate or House had time to read or comprehend much of the substance within it. And still the bill passed. One might say it was history in the making. It's a health care bill that makes me sick just thinking about it. Its making will go down in history—a historic tragedy that will forever blemish not health care but the process of moving bills through the House and Senate. In the future, health care and the American people may be looked at as victims of friendly fire.

Everyone that voted for that thing should have been relieved of duty for dereliction thereof because none of them read that damn thing.

Chapter 11:

No Bill Passed

*N*o bill passed by the House or the Senate should be much longer than a written page (and at most, twenty-five pages). That sounds reasonable. This rule would not only allow the men and women of the House and the Senate to read the bills, but it will also enable them to comprehend the substance of what they would be putting into law.

For example, sadly, as an American citizen I am totally unprepared to voice an intelligent opinion on the existing health care bill. But I am in good company, because neither can any House or Senate member. How could anyone digest that New-Jersey-sized phone book worth of craziness?

Chapter 12:

Our US Government Leadership

Have your children ever faked sick or told a lie in order to escape a day of school or cover up a little problem? Sure they have. The little rascals' voices and facial expressions as they tell the little sad tales are normally filled with doubt as they speak to you. The doubt comes from them thinking you might not believe the lines they are giving you. Well, guess what, politicians? Americans see the same kind of expressions of the faces of certain government officials on primetime television.

I think it was Abe Lincoln that said something to the effect of, "If I send you to buy a horse, I expect you to tell me about his points, not how many hairs he has in his tale." We are not as incapable of understanding as you think. You politicians go on and on in voluminous description of anything and everything except subject at hand. I may be an average American, but I can see a diversion and thoughts not pertaining to the real issues, and America is tired of it.

Some politicians can't say hello without a political spin attached (e.g., my wife and family thanks you, my dog thanks you, etc.). Pitiful. Just pitiful. Do us all a favor and just touch gloves and come out fighting for America. After viewing a 2008 presidential debate, the question in my mind was not which candidate I thought had the right stuff to lead this nation; instead I was empty, absolutely empty. I was so very disgusted. I couldn't find a firm leader among them.

What do we want from our president and House and Senate leadership? Read my lips: we want *honesty*. Bless his heart, George Bush Sr. had to eat his words on taxes during his term, but I love him anyway. President Bush Sr. decided to give it up on national television. It was a straightforward explanation, but at least honesty prevailed. Why isn't anyone apologizing for the handling of the health care bill or better yet, apologizing for the way the goddamn thing got ramrodded into existence. Hell, we Americans love our president, and none of us believed President Bush Sr. could have stopped taxes from being raised in the first place. But we knew he would try. We give all our presidents the benefit of the doubt that they will try. I even believed the one that smoked pot but didn't inhale. *Not.* Yes, I even love you, President Obama, even though you have reneged on so many of your campaign promises. I may not vote for you, but I still love you as my President.

Americans can't stand listening to the extreme Left or Right, for that matter. Actions are what it's all about. At least our presidents demonstrate action as they push ahead. I am not so sure about the House and the Senate. Those wolf packs have to find out what their political buddies say, forget what the people of the United State desire. Well, maybe the 2010 midterm elections taught some politicians a lesson about listening to the American people and what happens to those who ignore us.

But I am here to tell you that we the people must continue to flex our muscles, speak out, and demand to be heard. We must demand action on the real issues of the day, many of which are discussed in this very book.

Politicians should know that if it's hard a issue, if it's controversial, Americans will understand you voicing concerns in either direction, but for God's sake make a decision and stand by it, Change only if you find out you were wrong, we will understand that too. And most importantly, base that decision on the will of the people, not on the will of special interests or what the vote has in it for you. Hey guys, it is not hard to make the decision. All you have to do is listen to masses, yes those guys and gals you represent. Don't be afraid of special interest groups. Talk to the people and support their demands. That's not too much to remember.

What do you think? Talk straight to us. We all hate trying to figure out what the hell you're talking about, and most of the time when that happens, we become confused because you're busy avoiding the issue at hand as words flow from your mouth. We don't like asking ourselves how this knucklehead got from the opening subject to someplace out in left field. We don't want a pretty face. Again I revert back to a Marine corps saying: "Sure it's pretty, but can it fight?" We want a fighter—a champ, not a chump. We want truth and integrity in our government leadership. We want to see it in our leaders. We want to hear it from their mouths and see it in their actions. So you lose a few votes with your honesty and someone might not like your plan, but you'd have one and you'd stick to it. Why would you do it? *For the people!* And we would love you for it.

I don't have to agree with everything my president says, but I have to believe that his or her intentions for doing or saying whatever it is are based on doing the right thing for this nation and its people. Give it to us straight. You can even be funny with us. Americans love to laugh, and we love to see the hearts of our leaders. Where did you go, Ronald Ragan? We don't like name-calling or political backstabbing. I liked Mrs. Clinton's comment about why the guys were picking on her in the 2008 presidential debate. She said it was not because she was a woman; it was because she was ahead. To me that was quick, direct, and it shut down the talk thereafter; therefore, it was also a very effective remark. And she looked her opponents in the eyes when she said it. That was impressive to me, and by doing so she demonstrated that she had the right stuff, unlike a few of the men standing next to her. Now because I said that some of you are probably now accusing me of being a Democrat. Wrong, I am a candidate voter not necessarily a party voter.

Americans respond well to straight shooters, and we respond even better to candidates who talk about the real problems and real issues of the day, the tougher the better. One thing I didn't like about the televised name-calling at the debates was that certain individuals involved looked into the audience as they slammed the guy or gal next to them. Hey, look the person you're dragging through the mud in the eye, you coward. Show us some character, not showmanship. Male or female, black or white—damn it, I'm voting for the one who demonstrates character, sincerity, and honesty, and will reflective of the people.

People of America beware of conclusions drawn from the 2012 Republican debates (unless those conclusions came from thoughts of your own). The 2012 debates are truly something to watch. However, be careful how you evaluate the candidates. Don't let the media evaluate them for you. (and I say this again in this book , because this thought its so very important to me). I believe these debates are designed to kick dirt into the faces of the candidates rather than be utilized as an instrument for Americans across the Nation to view and listen to potential Presidential candidates.

One thing for sure, there are good people on those stages. Each one, however, have guns turned on them the minute that old liberal media gets a chance to adjust their fire. Mr. Romney, jerked around as a result of his religion: GOOD CANDIDATE. Governor Perry, jerked around because he had a bout of memory loss on stage at one point: another GOOD CANDIDATE. And I ask you, who has not lost a thought or had something similar happen to them in their lifetime? We all have. So, is Gov. Perry really a joke or is he just human? I suggest human and also a fine American as well as a very capable Presidential candidate. And what about Herman Cain? To me also a good candidate; many would vote for him on possibility of what his tax plan would do to the IRS(and that is dwindle it down to something manageable, and at the same time simplifying the way Americans pay taxes). Debates can't truly give you the man or woman as a President. They actually capture little of what these contenders have to offer that position. So why does the media cling to them the way they do? My thoughts are that they do so to show the world that they regulate the events of the day. These masters of manipulation are selling, and unfortunately many of us are buying their particular view for the day. They have recently destroyed Herman Cain. However, some would argue Herman's past destroyed him. But its funny former President Clinton can today voice opinions on any subject and the crowds are pleased to listen. Now as a President he openly lied about his misdoings yet old Herman is dead in the water from the allegations alone. (media power)

The Fact is these debates don't search the souls and can't bring the true strength of the candidates into view. They for the most part, attack the shortfall of the day and proceed to destroy the candidates along the way. *The fact is, in the end the media will select the non-Democrat candidate in the 2012 election, and it is very possible the least qualified person on the stage may win the crown. And if you don't think that can happen, then I would suggest you take a look at us now. (And then call me for your American Knucklehead Hat).*

Personally, I applaud every candidate. My advice to them would be to hang in there because Americans can get past religious affiliation, or that lapse of memory on stage or the fact that you represent a political party which is relatively new in our country's history (Tea Party). The fact is we can even get past a change in your thoughts from one direction to another. Hell, we get smarter, we gather better information; therefore we change our thoughts and at times our direction. The ones we can't stomach are those that refuse change. Particularly those that know they are wrong. I, like many other Americans, cannot stand those leaders who put the American people second to their individual needs and greed; those who sell out our Nation and its people by refusing to fight the real fight. **The former speaker has within him a wealth of knowledge. He has probably forgotten more than the President can remember about the workings of American politics, and the country itself for that matter.** I haven't checked the box yet but I Who ever I vote for will not be selected by the Media (He or She will be my choice).

Chapter 13:

Don't Get Old in America

The plight our elderly is sad. It's bad enough that as we grow older our bodies begin to fail us, but in this country, faltering health is only one of the obstacles an aging body faces. Being cared for when the faltering begins is another. The fact is that when we get old is the one time—if ever—the government should come to our aid in the form of entitlement care.

Free health care for the elderly and free prescriptions for the elderly—not a working person in this country would mind being taxed on behalf of an entitlement of that kind. But instead we are taxed for free phones, free or practically free housing (for endless in durations), and free food (the more babies you've got, the more of it you get). Free, free, *free*—all *unearned*.

I don't know about you, but I hurt for every American worker who has spent a lifetime working and struggling his or her way to retirement. And then once there, he or she is beaten into poverty by issues totally out of his or her control (e.g., health issues); this is normally the start of the downward spiral, followed by loss of a home and soon a loss of dignity, all as a result of paying astronomical prices for health services, prescription drugs, and the care relating to them.

Do we not realize that in those golden years is when most health issue appears? No hardworking American who has earned the right to retire should be subjected to having to pay out of his or her retirement or lose his or her home to stay alive. No American at this point in his or her life should have face losing it all just to stay alive.

Does it make a lot of sense that upon retirement from your workplace, the good health insurance that went with your job says bye-bye? It's simple: free health care and dental care for all Americans over the retirement age of sixty-five. They are to receive quality and complete health services at the expense of the United States government as a result of the taxes they have paid all their goddamn lives. And all prescriptions required to keep these Americans alive will be furnished free at the expense of pharmaceutical companies throughout the United States. Pharmaceutical companies will not be required to pay state or federal income tax as result of their unselfish contribution. Can you believe it? I just wrote a health care bill for the elderly of our country that fits on one page, with not one deceptive statement included and not one earmark.

Care for our elderly is one entitlement I can live with. Why? Because they are in fact entitled to it. I would rather pay for them than pay for someone who gained three hundred pounds just so they would fit the guidelines required to receive a government handout.

Back to the elderly; these citizens should not have to circle the globe to be seen and cared for. They shouldn't have to cross the border to pick up cheaper perceptions. No, it should be on the house, done so at the expense of tax dollars. Medical care should be an absolute for these very special Americans.

Excellence in health care in our nation should be part of the reward of working. You want me to pay taxes? I would do so happily for programs that care for America's elderly.

Chapter 14:

Education

Education. We talk about education from the standpoint of every American child having the right and need for an education that can offer him or her unlimited opportunities. The concept is golden and wonderful in theory; however, the fact is that every child doesn't possess the mental or physical ability to master unlimited ranges and scopes of curriculum. Yet from an education standpoint, we are all tossed into the same blender.

Let's face it. We are all not meant to be doctors. Some of us have mechanical minds, others of us have artistic minds, and still others of us have mathematical and scientific minds that may someday save the world through chemistry. However, whatever we are—firefighters, GIs, accountants, mechanics, or presidential candidates—we all have something to offer this nation. I believe there is pride in anyone who brings something to the table, in particular if one's heart and soul is consumed in the undertaking.

I think it was old Ben Franklin that said if we all think alike, then nobody is thinking. Every American has something to offer. Just because a kid can't comprehend algebra does not mean educating him or her from then on should focus only on graduation from high school, which would basically close the door to future dreams of higher education or other accomplishments, goals, and personal endeavors.

It seems to me that today's education system is not designed to tap into an individual's potential. It's more of an assembly line, and if folks are broken or injured along the way, the process will begin to overlook and eventually discard those who are unable to keep up. President Obama has reported through several media outlets that 30 percent of our high school students aren't graduating. And many who do graduate can't read or write at a twelfth-grade level. These nongraduates are discarded in the end, considered underachievers to a degree and destined to stand in the path of educational stagnation. After that, for the most part they join the ranks of a low or poor American lifestyle.

I believe identical education is necessary in the early stages of a child's development; children should go through a nonaltering basic corps or classes (hereafter referred to as BCC). The BCC should consist of reading skills, writing skills, and basic arithmetic skills (math to include adding, subtracting, multiplying, dividing, fractions, and decimals). BCC is the first step of the educational process, and it should never be compromised, for it will be the foundational base required to advance in the educational process. Each student should be tested with strict compliance to meet the mandatory learning objectives of the BCC.

Only after passing the BCC will students be allowed to move on to the next educational platform. The amount of time it takes to complete the BCC can change from student to student as a result of the student's scholastic ability. Time limits in form of semesters, days, months, and years it takes students to traverse through the BCC should not be based on a stringent calendar completion date. (Yes, set up the terms in semesters and years; however, the most important concept is that each student must meet and pass this requirement at this very basic level before he or she can move on.) The BCC is the foundational step that cannot be compromised, and it is the doorway to every kid's future hopes and dreams.

The next platform should include such things as basic US history and government courses, perhaps a basic Earth science focus, and some overview in the arts. Beyond this, all education should be employed through what could be known as educational pathways (or fields of study) and the associated classes. The length of time it took a student to complete the BCC will influence the pathway he or she enters at this point.

Children should have some input in finding their own pathways. And they should have desire and pride in its acceptance. For example, let's say a student chooses a culinary pathway. The culinary arts field of higher education features classes related to the wide topic of subject matter associated with culinary arts (e.g., everything from food preparation to restaurant management). This particular education field will allow a student wide range of employment opportunities, everything from being a chef to being an owner/manager of a restaurant or catering business, etc.

The idea of the various fields is to allow individuals avenues to target their employment dreams. Education themes can expand to many worthwhile trades, including anything from law enforcement to the practice of law. Educational pathways could also be called dream makers.

All jobs and professions have pathways. And in the end everyone fits and becomes a productive member of our society. Today, the education system needs to focus on making individuals professional at what they do and opening doors for all kinds of employment;

however, they should also direct students toward a path of professional acceptance for their desired profession.

However, the beginning of any and all educational searches must start with a firm grasp of the BCC. A youngster unable to read, write, and perform basic math requirements is lost early on in today's educational programs and found twelve years later unable to read and write. He or she graduates high school with little hope for a future. These days, the kids at this point for the most part become members of national dependencies.

How many high school graduates today cannot perform these basic skills at the twelfth-grade level? The numbers are high, staggeringly high, even frighteningly so. We can change that by concentrating on the basic elementary learning skills early on and not allowing those basic skill requirements to be compromised in the educational process.

If it takes a bit longer for some, so be it, for without those skills, life's dreams fade away fast. And so does a child's opportunity for happiness, self-worth, and financial success.

Chapter 15:

Violence in America

In January 2011 in Arizona, an act of violence killed a beautiful nine-year-old child and laid to rest several others just as important to our society and loved by families and friends; the same act seriously wounded others, including a beloved member of the United States House of Representatives.

What should have taken place just hours after the killings is this man should have been blindfolded, strapped to a pole next to a wall, and shot and executed by a firing squad. I think as a nation our laws are failing us. Our prisons do nothing more than allow the most dangerous of our society a place to continue their terror and make themselves even more dangerous to society each day they are incarcerated. What is cruel and unusual is that our society will lock up a nonviolent prisoner with society's most ruthless, violent killers and rapists. Why? Because prisons are overcrowded. People who have killed on the outside continue to rape, kill, and pillage within the confines of state and federal correctional institutes. Now that's cruel.

That's right, these ruthless bastards are at helms in our prisons, and everything they touch is destroyed or made worse. Execute them; execute them *all*. You bleeding hearts that cry out at my words, the reason you object is because you look at these killers as someone's son or daughter. I look at them for what they are: monsters and rabies-infected animals that kill, rape, and pillage our society. However, most importantly, I also look at them for what they have done to someone else's sons and daughters, and they have done so with little to no remorse and no emotion whatsoever. And once locked up, some of them continue their rampages behind bars.

It sounds terrible, this talk of taking criminals' lives, but this practice is the only one that could penetrate that cruel world and put an end to the problem: firing squads to each of them, complemented by the prison population and nation population being able to view the executions. What, do you think it would be too much for television? Come on, give me a break. Today's motion picture industry and the television sets in our homes have much to do with the rise of violence and crime in this nation. And if you don't believe that, get in line to receive your American Knucklehead Hat.

Why not let television contribute to the cure? Trust me, that is one reality program that would be widely viewed. If you don't believe the movie industry contributes to a violent America, then you, my little naive friend, are an idiot. Violence in the theaters, in video games, in music—these things have promoted violence across the nation in many ways, combined with a system of law that fails to punish, prevent, and deter violence.

Face it. Our laws are very abstract, without balance in many cases. In this day and age, a parent sticking a bar of soap in a kid's mouth (you remember the old cure for bad language) would result in a child abuse charge. Imagine a parent being jailed for that. But on the other hand, we will feed and prevent murdering bastards from being punished by death. Can't you see that we are out of touch with justice these days? We overreact to the nonsensical whims of the few and underreact in the punishment of the violent and deadly criminals in our land.

If you don't believe that, step up and get your knucklehead hat. Hell, take two.

Chapter 16:

Close the Doors

I am tired of hearing foreign nations belittling America. While Egypt's government was in turmoil, I listened to Egypt's vice president downplaying the American government and our form of democracy. He didn't mind the resemblance when his country was being fed one weapon system after another.

Get ready, America. This particular Arab nation is armed to the *t* with some of the best military weapons America has to offer, including aircraft, tanks, and missiles. These same weapons have all the bells and whistles in them to make them extremely deadly and accurate. Who the hell armed them? Hell, we did. We are our worst enemy doing things like that. Wait, not *we*—our government.

Talk about irony. Our government plans to cut military spending in 2012, yet we continue arm/outfit questionable allies like Egypt. What sense do you see in such actions? We all know the real question at this point is if the Muslim Brotherhood will be in the driver's seat in Egypt as this chapter of history ends. The same kind of turnover is taking place with the Gaddafi regime this very day. Be careful. In the end it might look like a democracy, but who's really driving the cart is the big question. We may not truly find out the answer until years down the road. God knows that more problems are just around the corner.

Now, I have to ask you, why we do the things that we do? Feed them weapons and buy that overpriced oil? I say close America's doors to any and all nations that pose even a hint of a threat to this country. Can we really trust the Arab nations as a whole in this day and age? Can we trust the Muslim Brotherhood to contribute anything to America's future except overpriced oil and a sincere hatred of our people and beliefs?

Do we not know that these people, for the most part, can't stand us? Do we not know these people? Look at the cowardly crowd that raped the British news girl. Don't I wish I could put a bullet into every one who participated in that cowardly act? Do I sound mean to some of you? If so, I truly don't care. Fanatics kill and rape in front of our eyes; people burn our flag with one hand and take our money and our weapons with the other; and people continuously preach anti-American rhetoric. What's our response? We continue to sell weapons to these volatile nations and reduce size of our military, reduce its budget, and sign nuclear treaties with the Russians. These same Arab countries screw with our economy with over-priced oil, holding us hostage. I believe they would happily use those weapons we gave them against us if the condition was to their advantage. We are so fucked up that the only true friend we have in that sand box is Israel, and our government is letting go of her hand.

I believe the best way to heal our economy is to close the doors. And more importantly, stop giving and selling weapons to the people who truly can't stand us. Do you hear me, American government? Stop putting weapons of destruction in the hands of these Arab nations. I don't care if they are smiling at you that day, and I don't give a damn about Arab oil. *Find oil elsewhere.*

Think about this, America: we build within this nation of ours, and we sell products to our people. We make products and price them so our people can buy them. Car manufacturers, if you want to build cars outside this nation, then I suggest you sell every one of those piece-of-shit cars outside the country as well. You bastards build them outside the country for pennies on the dollar and then you bring them back here and sell them to your American brethren for two hundred times what you have in them. You all need to go to hell. American entrepreneurs are ready to take your place. We don't need you.

I would rather buy an auto with technology of the thirties than buy a new modern American auto built in China. Yes, our food, our machinery, our automobiles, and our energy sources should all be manufactured and gathered here in the good old USA. And all of it should be used to feed and care for our own population—a working population. We should live and breathe America. We need to put to work those Americans who have forgotten how to work or who have never had the opportunity.

Do you realize that we are the only nation on Earth that can get away with that idea in today's world? I know there are people out there who would say we couldn't maintain our economy with resources from within our own nation. The fact is we can; the fact is we have done it before. It may not be easy at first, and there may have to be great sacrifice in the beginning, but I just know it could be done.

Remember how we gained our independence in the first place. You all remember that, don't you? We can be independent of nations around the world, particularly those that are dangerous to us and make dangerous statements about alienating and/or destroying those people they consider inferior by race and religion.

By God, it's just the right time to be independent of those type of nations, and once America pulls away from every country around us that has burned our flag, cursed our people, and killed our GIs, they will all see just how powerful our nation is. And at the same time, we Americans will realize just how much we don't need them. *We don't need the world to survive; we need only the will of the American people.* Think about the jobs that would materialize. Think about the powerful nation that would grow.

Lastly, we should continue to partner with friends from all countries that respect us as we respect them.

Chapter 17:

American Prisons

Our prisons have become warehouses of the most dangerous animals ever to take the form of human beings. And what do we do? We do nothing. Our laws and criminal process cannot match the terror and punishment these animals deliver to the weak in their lives every day.

Prisons don't deter these foul examples of human life. Prisons provide barbells to make these bastards larger, stronger criminals. Prisons are entertainment facilities for the cruel—facilities that allow them to kill, maim, batter, and sexually abuse the weak confined with them. If anything, prisons make prisoners more ruthless, uglier, and more evil before they exit the system down the road. The fact that prisons across the nation are overcrowded is the biggest contributing factor to early releases. Think about that.

Take away the TVs and the Internet; let these people entertain themselves with hard work, growing their own food. Remove the toys, the Internet, the barbells, etc., or is such removal of toys for those who kill and rape too cruel and unseemly for you that you would lobby for them? And lastly, above all make prison life a horrible, awful memory. Make it an experience never to be forgotten. Do not make it this way with abuse or by allowing other prisoners with the upper hand to torment and abuse; but instead make it unforgettable with physical isolation and work crews, and get control of the prisoners' minds and bodies. For example, isolation would not only protect them from each other inside, but it would also make them look forward to a return to society, if that was in the cards for them.

I say that people who killed in crime should be executed. We know prison can't cure them, so they must be completely removed from the society they threaten. Punishment to fit the crime: I just know I have heard that statement before. Have you? And what, may I ask, is cruel or unusual about executing a killer? *Not a thing.* Now, I am not talking about accidental homicides (e.g., car accidents, etc.). I am talking about rapist killers, murdering spouse killers, the gang killers, drive-by killers, etc. Let's stop spending money protecting other nations' borders in lands far away and build prisons in our land to house these demons and dregs of society. And more importantly, let's kill those who must be destroyed.

As for the nonviolent criminals, once they are locked up, make them serve the sentence imposed; do not parole them after a small portion of the time served. Put each of them in a small room with a toilet, a sink, and a shower built into the corner of the cell. Allow them no contact with fellow prisoners, and serve them MREs—ready-to-eat meals specially designed for a prison setting (e.g., meals with a cardboard knife and fork). Or make them eat like the Arabs, with their hands (but don't tell them about that left-hand business in eating; let them figure that out for themselves).

Give them books to entertain themselves, preferably something to stimulate the mind educationally and aimed at career building. But always remember, they have been incarcerated to be *punished.*

Punishing criminals, that's the key. The fact is our GIs in many places live harder than many prisoners live in today's jails. You want to talk about close quartering and cruel living conditions, ask any enlisted navy man how much space he was afforded while on board naval vessels. They are elbow to elbow and sometimes stacked on top of each other four or five tall. For junior officers, it's four to a stateroom, which is the size of a small bathroom with one sink. Or ask a Marine, who's toilet is where he digs it.

What's really crazy is the thought of letting prisoners reign as criminals with a criminal hierarchy within the walls of a prison. Is that not insane? And that is exactly what every documentary of today's prisons depicts. My God, convicts have chains of command within prison gangs, etc. That does not sound like a good thing. They kill, rape, and brutalize each other within the prison facilities, within the walls/instrument designed to take freedom from them. They prey on the weak just like they did in the society that locked them up. So what the hell are they learning? *Nothing.*

Execute those violent bastards. Remove them from the surface of the Earth before the walls fall down completely in the American penal system. Now to me, the brutal things they do to each other are cruel and very unusual and do nothing to prepare them to be released from the prison should the time come. The system did nothing more than make them meaner and uglier.

In Saudi Arabia, if a man is tried and convicted of being a thief, the law says the authorities can cut off his hand. It seems a little cruel and unusual to me as an American. However, in those countries with crimes and punishment as stated above have very few repeat offenders. It's said if a man is convicted of rape, they don't cut off the hand; they cut off the weapon used in the assault. You can bet that would lessen the chance of that crime being repeated (by that person anyway).

As Marines, after the war end, some of my pals and I drove to a city. I remember we were in the kingdom of Saudi Arabia. We bought groceries and left them on the sidewalk outside the store unattended while we walked several blocks over to get our vehicle. The storekeeper said it would be okay to do that. When we returned, our groceries were right where we left them on the sidewalk in front of the store. Show me any place, any store in America where you could do that day after day, in particular if the store was located within close vicinity to government housing.

I am not saying that we should follow the laws of that kingdom. But I am saying we must stop the violence in our country, and maybe adopting one or two of their laws wouldn't be so bad. Putting to death those who kill would be a *great start*, particularly if it helps rid us of the most violent criminals.

Prisoners should have no rights; once incarcerated, they should not be protected by American law for crimes that take place behind bars. Those involved in acts of violence performed in the confines of state and federal prisons should be disciplined by rule of the prison, rule with stern and—if need be—indifferent laws and punishments that do not pertain to common citizens on the outside. I know what you bleeding hearts are saying: the prison authorities would become corrupt, and punishment would get out of hand. Hell, the prisoners now are in control, and they are corrupt and very much out of hand. This must end. Do you have a better suggestion? Sorry, a time-out won't work.

The prisons should be the first centers of punishment those who violate the rules of society, *not just places to house them.* Rehabilitation always needs to be second to that. I know you pantywaist bureaucrats don't like the idea of executing those savages, but I guarantee mainstream America does. Oh that's right, you don't give a damn what mainstream America wants.

Chapter 18:

Teachers—Hail to Miss Crabtree

oday's heroes—teachers fit well into this category. They are completely underrated for their overall importance to this country's future. Teachers care for our kids in a society where both kids and parents can and do abuse them at times. With tied hands, they just continue to march. These child-loving Americans graduate from colleges and universities throughout our land; they nurture and groom the most important seeds America plants; and on average, they make one-forth the salary of American auto workers. But fear not. Teachers unions will come to the rescue and destroy teachers as they have the auto workers and any other occupation they put their greedy hands on. Before you know it, you will be out of a job altogether and America will be sending our children to China to be educated (educated by the Chinese at a ten-cents-an-hour wage).

Don't get me wrong. I believe there is a disparity in the way teachers are paid, retired, and cared for from a health care perspective. And if you don't believe that, ask any auto worker (or should I say any former auto worker). I am not saying the auto workers of America do not deserve a decent wage. No, what I am saying is that the teachers of our children, in this day and age in particular, deserve it just as much, if not more. Today's teachers have more to contend with in the classroom than just the business of teaching. Teachers today have to tend to the most undisciplined youths ever to traverse the halls of education establishments. And if you don't believe that, then look back and ask yourself how many police and security personnel roamed the halls of your middle school when you were a kid.

Teachers work with the most undisciplined society of youth ever to hit the streets of America. Yes, students today can and are at times abusive to them. Some on these kids are on drugs, some are violent, and so many are downright disrespectful. Today's teachers are cursed at, and at times they are physically abused, yet these heroes stay in the educational arena. And do we help? Hell no, we don't. We tie the hands of these men and women that teach our children. Our children get into trouble, and we stand beside our kids and blame everything and everyone but ourselves and our kids. Do we tan our kids' hides when they are young like our daddies did? Hell no, we don't. If we did, we would risk the chance of being turned in for child abuse. Is there something not balanced about all this to any of you?

Prisons don't punish, and parents can't discipline their children for fear of injustice at the hands of local authorities. It's all coming back. *The walls are falling.* Not really, not yet. It's ridiculous but true. Parents are too frightened spank their children's bottoms. What is wrong with that picture? It's about control again; this time parents lose control, and they do so at the hands of the government and lawmakers.

Speaking of parental control, do you believe the ACLU is promoting the taking of a school girl across state lines to have an abortion? No parental consent necessary. I don't see anyone locking these SOBs up. Go ahead and take my child across a state line to do such a thing, and I promise no law, no police department, no army would stop me from taking you apart piece by piece.

America's walls—what do you think? Up, down, or shaking about? I think you can spank a kid without abusing them. That's why God put those pillowlike cushions in their rears. Teachers can be cursed at, struck, called terrible names in front of the entire class, and their only recourse is to asked this enraged little person to please leave and go to the principal's office. Like that is going to work. Teachers have no armor or means to protect themselves. The government took it all away with laws that made them vulnerable and incapable of protecting themselves and preserving order in their classrooms.

Prior to taking a heavily fortified objective and prior to leaving the assembly area, Marines are told to surrender all weapons. A Marine might have second thoughts concerning the mission. However, Marine leadership would never put those brave warriors into that kind of situation. So why do we make laws that fail to protect the teachers and leave them totally defenseless?

Student abuse of teachers should have consequences. One witness should be all a teacher needs to confirm the account. And if it gets down to he said she said, then the teacher should *always* be given the befit of the doubt. Fines should be levied on the students' parents. Set fines for every level of abuse. If a student talks back to a teacher once, a ten-dollar fine should be imposed on the parents. If a student curses at a teacher, a fifty-dollar fine should be imposed on the parents. Students who would put their hands on a teacher should be given a mandatory suspension of thirty days, and a two-hundred-dollar fine should be imposed of the parents.

Why make the parent pay? Well, the problem did not begin in the classroom. Parents, take responsibility for your young ones. I can guarantee one thing: if kids' behavioral problems hit home by causing fines to be levied on the parents, attitude adjustments will take place *fast*. Kids' attitudes will change for the better rapidly. Parents will begin to intervene, and bad behavior will be corrected. This discipline and fine-levying system needs to roll out across all school-related activities (e.g. bus rides to and from school, etc.).

Protect the teachers, and gain control of the school house so they can educate our youth. Get that switch out, Miss Crabtree, and you parents support the use of it. Trust me on this one. The only people in this land who would not agree with this last thought are those who don't have control of their children. For the most part, Americans parent well and demand discipline within their households. Therefore, I say forget all you special-interest whiners. And shame on you parents who can't see the wrong in your children back talking and being abusive to teachers.

Chapter 19:

Special-Interest Whiners

America likes whiners the same way we like weak handshakes and kids that wear their pants hanging off their asses. Special-interest whiners are people and groups that blame others for their problems and or downfalls. They suck up to discriminators of all kinds; race, religion, economy, antipatriots, or anybody with a damn cause. These whiners normally prey on issues and think problem solving has to do with monetary help and assistance; however, in reality only the few gain from the action taken.

The will of the American people is constantly being chipped away as the little voices of these self-interest whiners win battle after battle. Whiners' justifications are always propelled by a selfish prize; sadly, many times their wins represent losses to our nation's early set of values and vision for its people.

Self-interest whiners feed off the fact America's leaders today are unable to say enough is enough. Their subject matter is diverse; topics range from attacks belittling, perverting, and/or misleading the writings of the US Constitution, forbiddance of prayer in schools, preparing the groundwork for a world of unearned, dangerous, and wasteful entitlements, one after another. However, American legislators should have never entertained most of the whiners' topics of concern in the first place, and they should have openly condemned the subjects as they entered the room. Nonetheless, whiners win constantly. For example, I realize the words "In God We Trust" were not printed on America's earliest forms of currency; however, it galls me that self interest groups fought to have these words removed from all of today's currency. However, they succeded only in having it removed from certain coins. Doing so at the expense of a nation of people whose voice was not respected in the overall outcome.

The win was justified only by the voice of the few, and that, my friends, is the same formula that is destroying the foundation of America in nearly every controversial, minority-centered demand.

In this particular episode (the "In God We Trust" removal), did we forget our forefathers' dedication to religious freedom? To these men, God was not a discriminating issue but rather the fabric that bound the nation together. Throughout our history, brave men and women have given their lives in defense of such ideals. So I ask you, who the hell cares what the self-interest whiners bring to the table to the contrary?

The framers of our Constitution *intended* God to be in the midst of everything this nation stands for, and no group with in this nation today—regardless of their presentation—should be able to override an issue by distorting our forefathers' constitutional intent, especially when the intent is so very clear. And you politicians and lawmakers who can't say no or who feel the need to protect votes by refraining from getting involved in such issues, well let's hope God never changes his mind concerning your future or your well-being.

Beware, America: the ACLU and organizations like ACORN are not finished

Chapter 20:

Entitlement Abuse

What a great topic for a presidential debate. Most Americans believe the largest wasteland of the American economy today lends itself to a theme of wasteful dollars being scattered about in unwarranted, abused, and unearned entitlements. The framers of our nation would roll over in shame if they knew this country had turned into land of handouts. Entitlements are often disguised by their good intentions; it's only after years of wasted dollars that the good ideas and good intentions are recognized for what they really are: centers for fraud, waste, and abuse of American tax dollars.

The word *entitlement* gives one the feeling that entitlement is something of a demand that our government must surrender. Entitlements are in some cases earned, such as Social Security; they are earned by mandatory contributions extracted from that individual's paycheck and, in the case of Social Security, placed into a nest egg for the entire time he or she works. Don't get me going on what the government does with that money while it's in the nest.

Sadly, however, not all entitlements are paid for and/or earned by the individual like in the case of Social Security. The unearned entitlements are the ones that working middle-class America *hate*. These particular entitlements are often the most abused and wasteful, and they are the same ones in which corruption at the hand of the users flows openly and is widely spread across the land.

These types of entitlements are looked at as handouts by us, the middle class, bought and paid for by hard-working American hands. And the people who continuously live off of them and promote their use to others (at times with great deception) are lowlife Americans.

Did you know that approximately half of America pays *no taxes*? Worried about the walls? Maybe just a little? Much of the half that give nothing will do all they can to keep it that way. Entitlements that offer no end are absolutely hated by working America, and you politicians out there better start recognizing that.

Unearned entitlements are bankrupting this country. Today's American government makes it too easy to live off of it, and it demands nothing from those who take advantage of the gifts given. This must end.

Chapter 21:

Handouts

Giving handouts doesn't improve the social conditions of the poor. Hasn't anyone figured that out except you and me? The United States government spends dollar after dollar, year after year on such programs, and the only thing that improves is the odds that more people will eventually meet the criteria for acceptance into the programs.

The best way to eliminate and lessen the use of these wasteful entitlement programs is very simple: make the users pay it back in one form or another (whether on a monetary basis or through work provided). Trust me, that will curb the waste immediately. And if you really want to cut it down, drug test the participants. (We will talk about that very subject next chapter.)

Back to this chapter's subject: handouts. The answer lies in reforming some of the existing entitlement program laws and doing away with the rest. (Did you hear? *Do away with the rest*). Has our government really not figured out that all of this is costing taxpayers money and making life harder on the American working class? And we are tired of it.

That's right. Average working men and women throughout the land believe government entitlements that are not earned should end after a period of time. We believe money given through entitlements should be earned or paid back, even if just a percentage of it is paid back, and with little exception.

Acceptable exceptions to the payback rule might include those who are incapable of working, have physical or mental handicaps, and who are elderly (people who are at an age that they cannot provide such return), in particular those elderly who worked and paid taxes all their working lives. It's time for them to take their packs off.

The problem is that today's American government makes it easy for people to live off of it. Or better said, today's government makes it easy to live off middle-class Americans. That's right, we middle-class working people make up the majority of that half of Americans who pay taxes.

Chapter 22:

Mandatory Drug Testing for Entitlement Users

Mandatory drug testing for participants in entitlement programs offered by this nation needs to be a mandatory ingredient in the application phase as well throughout the entire time a recipient receives compensation (through the form of random drug tests).

Do you know any American who would disagree with that statement? Oh, excuse me. Do you know any hard-working American *taxpayer* who would disagree with that statement? Can our government not see? Yes, they see; they just refuse to act on it because of the tremendous controversy relating to this particular issue and I belive as well they don't react in fear of uncovering a truly large population of offenders. You know, the irony of these situations is that welfare office employees across the country are required to take drug tests, as are those who are employed as public housing staff, yet the those who are awarded with program dollars are not tested and there is no requirement that they be tested. What's wrong with this picture?

God knows American workers would go along with drug testing these folks. What's wrong with you politicians? Do you not realize that we are the ones who sent you to Capitol Hill? We expect—no, we demand—that you look out for the well-being of the nation. We demand that you stop passing bills that do not honor the will of the people. Making difficult decisions is part of the job.

Chapter 23:

Term Limits

A lifetime spent serving in Senate or House seats is noble, wouldn't you say? At the same time, it can be dangerous. I believe the preponderance of these men and women enter office with an unselfish desire to do well for the nation or their state—good intentions all the way. And then time sets in, and as time passes, these fine Americans—some with total disregard and others who are just unaware—have a tendency to remove themselves from the people they represent.

They are removed not only in form of distance at times but also in the form of obligation to the people who elected them into that prestigious office. The constant travel, the dinners, the meetings and soon they are more likely to be listening and responding to lobbyists and other special interests who continuously position themselves nearby, and in these people the lawmakers see opportunity that may or may not be representative of those who elected them and at times might even be an individual opportunity. After all, they see and hear from lobbyists and special interest groups far more than they see and hear from their constituents (the people they truly represent). Some of the distraction is a necessary evil (gathering facts, etc.); however, after too much time away from the voters, these people get lost in politics and lose track of the very people they represent.

It was disturbing to me to hear of a very senior senator refer to what he described as "freshman" in a way that suggested that their voices meant nothing, that this group of newly elected senators basically has nothing to say; they need follow only. *Bullshit.*

On the other side of the issue, the lack of term limits allows our statesmen and stateswomen to mature into their roles and allows them to educate themselves along the way so that they can in time become better statespeople—the role they were elected to serve.

By the way, maturing into a role is one thing, but disrespecting/discarding their constituents' opinions along the way is conceit (and *bad politics*).

In conclusion, a term limit to me is a good thought. However, their term should not last forever; perhaps it should last just long enough to get them back in touch with the people and the conditions and times within their home states, whatever that amount of time may be.

Chapter 24:

Our Flag

Over half of the medals of honor awarded in the American Civil war were awarded to flag bearers. In the battle of Fredericksburg alone, thirteen men were killed, each clinging to the flag he gallantly retrieved from the dead or wounded bearer before him. The original flag bearer himself entered the battle armed with only a flag in his hands. My God, can you imagine that?

I wonder what any one of those thirteen men would do in response to seeing the burning of our flag by a war protester or a member of the Arab nations, or an article group within. At the same time, how would they react to the thought of forbidding the pledge of allegiance to that same flag in classrooms across the nation? The American flag is more than a symbol of our nation. It is our nation's history at a glance. It represents the pride, patriotism, and honor that the nation holds within it. It represents the will and honor of the greatest nation ever founded. A nation under God, not to mention with liberty, justice, and freedom for all. These words should send chills of pride up the spine of every true American. Our flag and allegiance to it is nothing more than a display of allegiance to our nation and its people. This type of allegiance should enter our children's thoughts as early in life as they can process them.

I know there is some idiot out there interpreting what I am saying with visions of training the Hitler youth; I am not saying anything of the kind. I would like to see our youth respect our past by respecting symbols like our flag, along with other things like national monuments, etc. I desire our children to be able to pledge allegiance to our flag and sing our national anthem without stumbling through the words. I would like them to envision the majesty of our history from the time of its conception through the difficult periods (e.g., the Revolutionary War, the Civil War, the attack on Pearl Harbor, and the hardships and triumphs of the civil rights movement—and yes—straight on through to the pride in American as we elected our first black president). Can anyone besides me see the value in such thought? Can anyone besides me see the greatness in our country? Sure you can.

And I ask you, what is wrong with an American heart hurting when an American flag is being burned on national television or an American heart hurting over movement to take God out of the pledge of allegiance (or for that matter, certain groups' desire to remove the pledge all together)?

Man, if we as a nation don't start to pledge our allegiance to this great country of ours very soon, we may find the changes that will follow so destructive that we won't recognize and won't be able to even see America after the smoke clears. I don't feel America is a second-rate country. I will never believe that. I have traveled to many areas of the globe, and for those of you who haven't, let me say that America is by far the greatest nation and country of all, and we all need to start believing in her as such. We need to stop the special interest insanity and start building American patriots once again.

It is always a special interest or some lobbying group that places its ugly, destructive hand on America's strength, that tear downs our values. These special interests and selfish lobbyists are America's kryptonite; they draw the strength and the good out of our nation anyplace they show up.

For example, the American Civil Liberties Union sued a public school district over the matter of the pledge of allegiance. What idiot came up with justification to prevent this little patriotic ritual? Can't we all see one of the things that fails this nation is its lack of commitment to maintaining our heritage and teaching sharing our history with our children? Our schools need to truly concentrate on US history and civics classes. I wonder how Betsy Ross would feel to see several piece-of-shit Arab men burning our flag and raping a news woman in the streets of their country. By the way, three cheers for the Arab women who so bravely interceded and stopped the rape from continuing. In closing, God bless our country and its flag. Three cheers for the red, white, and blue.

Chapter 25:

The American Constitution

The American Constitution is the blueprint of America's beliefs. How can any member of this country's Senate or House make statements alluding to a lack of concern for what that document says? These guys are our nation's lawmakers. Do they not realize that all laws in this nation must conform to what that particular document says? God forbid the remaining lawmakers follow in that sort of thinking.

Members of the Continental Congress that helped draft the Constitution must be turning over in their graves as these nonbelievers and nonconformists assume office. To me, comments that express disregard for that particular document are not just disgraceful, but they are treasonous as well. My God, the document is the framework of our beliefs as Americans. The same document has been the verbal and written outline/blueprint for the birth of democracies across the world.

Our US Constitution, Bill of Rights, and Declaration of Independence are more than words on paper; they represent the inherent beliefs of the framers of our country, our country's forefathers, and generation after generation to follow. What's all this negative talk about these documents in this day and age? It speaks volumes about the quality of some of today's American leaders.

People make jokes about that today. But the fact is that the Constitution's words represent what we were and still are, despite the negative words of some of this country's leadership. Those who would laugh or think nonsensical, funny, or other degrading thoughts toward to the United States Constitution need to get the heck out of this country. We don't need you, and we damn sure don't need you holding a seat in the legislative branch.

The Constitution and the Bill of Rights are the heart and soul of America, the strength and wisdom of our nation, and the basis for all laws written in our land. But don't tell that to the ACLU. They rip into and distort its meaning for the sake of any cause or disgruntled group that comes along with a greedy, selfish interest, and they put those causes and groups into the media's eyes. If anything needs dismantling, it's the ACLU. Don't worry about me showing up at your damn meetings; you people disgust me. I won't be there.

Lastly, men and women sacrificed bravely and with great honor to move this country on the right path; they fought gallantly for the freedoms these documents represent. America, don't let any organization or any part of our government or any self-interest group minority, business, religious group, union, or form of perverted leadership lessen their importance or distort US Constitution from the original meaning those who wrote it intended.

Chapter 26:

Tax Dollars—America's Nightmare

It is bad enough that American tax dollars are garnished from Americans' incomes, but to have our government misuse and abuse these funds is disgraceful. Tax dollars being ill spent, misused, and abused is without question one of the biggest factors in the fall of the dollar. We in the middle class have watched our federal and state governments' careless handling of these dollars, and we're at the point where we are not only sick of it but embarrassed as well.

Our debt ceiling is so high, it now reaches into to the ozone. I just figured it out! The environmentalists, those tree-hugging idiots, have been wrong all along. It's the debt ceiling penetrating the ozone and making holes in it. That talk of greenhouse gases they have been slinging is just a bunch of bullshit.

Our tax dollars are being flushed into the holes; yes, we don't have to look hard to see the holes of corruption and wastelands of misuse in entitlements, one after another. And they always seem to be serving the same self-serving degenerates that live off their fellow men. Yes, Americans are more than disgruntled about their tax dollars being misused. We are heartbroken with every news bulletin that exposes the corruption. Billions upon billions upon *billions* wasted in programs filled with waste and fraud, as well as programs with no ends attached to them.

And that's not mentioning the billions of tax dollars spent to care for illegal immigrants that cause economic chaos on a daily basis at the state and federal levels. America protects borders around the globe, why not its own? Americans watch their hard-earned tax dollars fly out the window all directions. And we the American middle class pay for that waste. And we are so very tired of footing that bill!

The tax dollar's original intent was to pay off a war debt. Question: did it ever get paid? Oh boy, has government expanded that original intent to include everything from bailing out banks to free phones (I have been told that one has resulted in some drug dealers having two and three phones). Taxes now span any and everything the government feels it need stick its hand into. Is that crazy or what? American taxes began to pay off war debt, and now Americans are consumed by taxes that pay for anything and everything. The government's tax base should be titled the *infinity tax*—tax collecting to the tune of a never-ending need.

Most Americans believe the dollar is taxed to the tune of about sixty cents on a dollar—state and federal totals, sales tax, groceries, etc. I think 60 percent may be a bit low. In a nutshell, our government has taken on far too many responsibilities, and far too many of them are not aligned to the government's real purpose. This is the formula that is destroying the nation it serves. I think someone needs to tell the president there is a difference between a capitalistic nation and a capitalistic government.

Chapter 27:

The Tea Party

I want to begin by saying I am not a Tea Party member. But I sure do admire the role the Tea Party has played in politics recently. The movement stands for reform, going back to the basics of government, cherishing our Constitution, fighting for the will of the people, and they in many cases are the only party that embraces the will of the masses. Think about it. They in many ways see the middle class (in particular, the working middle class) with clearer vision than any other party. Heck, I don't know why I am not a member. Who knows, by the next presidential election, I may be.

To them, our forefathers are not a joke; instead, they believe the Founding Fathers represent all that is good in our nation's character. I may not be a Tea Party member, but the Tea Party is very much a part of me as I view the country in this day and age. Truly this political party is a breath of fresh air in today's world of politics.

Some of the national media paint this group as conservative extremists. I paint them a bit more colorfully than that; I paint them as patriots. And I believe they exist for all the right reasons. Frankly, I can't find a lot of wrong in people who question the politics of today. Damn it, if anything deserves questions poked at it, it would be the politics of *today*. Know that I applaud them. I can't blame any American for not wanting to be part of the voice of America. (That's why I wrote this book. I too want a voice in America's future, and I believe it's my right as an American to be able to voice it.)

It's the right of all the citizens of our country, and it's the missing piece of the pie in today's America. Most importantly, the Tea Party has and is becoming a powerful tool in the selection of men and women seeking political office, and what's really neat about them is that they have done so by embracing both the cause of democracy and the people of our nation at the same time.

Their contributions thus far, I believe, reflect America in its purest form. They are nonviolent yet no nonsense in their approach to service and in the selection of those they support as their representatives. No, I can't find a lot of bad in this group. Hell, I can't find *any* bad in them. I see a great deal of good in America's future thanks to their efforts. On the other hand, how many Democrat and Republican supporters can look at their parties with true affection based on the belief that they will rally around the needs of the people? *Not!* I have to admit, I love and will never forget Ms. Martin's words as she stood up and shouted, "Congress, can you hear us now?" in the aftermath of the midterm elections that changed the look of the House and Senate.

God bless the Tea Party. I would like them even more if they would gather up Harry Reed and toss him into the Boston Harbor for a little swim. Maybe some of the tea would give him a little color. But make sure a lifeguard is available because I'd bet he can't swim, and I wouldn't want him to get hurt.

Chapter 28:

American Patriotism

Don't be ashamed of your patriotism. Be proud of it. Americans, be even more proud to display it!

As a younger man I use to love to watch President Reagan speak. He made us proud to be Americans. In my time, he was the only president that made you feel that way every time he opened his mouth. He boldly and bravely spoke out against evil empires. Damn it, he spoke out, and he never let the world get confused as to the strength and power of our nation. He *never* talked of our nation being second rate in anything. That's right; words suggesting we were second to any other nation would have never come from his mouth. *He didn't believe it*, and more importantly, he didn't sell it.

And for as long as he was our president, no American questioned America's strength and resolve in any situation and even more importantly, its overall power. The US hostages were released as Reagan entered office. Anyone care to take a guess as to why? The answer is that Ronald Regan and his administration would have turned Iran into the world's largest kitty litter box on the face of the Earth, and if you don't believe that, I am sure there are some knucklehead hats left. How many of you believe the current administration would have been able to walk into that situation and had Iran respond in the same way?

Our beautiful history has millions upon millions of names we could add to the list of patriots—people who loved our nation without reservation. We need to make sure those names are followed by more names, more than ever before. America is a great nation (the greatest nation of *all*).

The president, every member of the House, and every member of the Senate need to say it, and most importantly, they need to believe it. By God, that alone would change the face of our nation today. That alone would be the key to resurrecting the political parties of this country.

Be proud to be an American, and remember that the people of today who have a problem with patriotism are the same people who have problem with God, our Constitution, and religious freedoms, and why? I think it has something to do with what John Adams said long ago, something about our Constitution being the work of a moral and religious people and it is inadequate to a government of any other. John Adams was quite a patriot himself, wouldn't you say? And a pretty smart guy at that.

Patriotism and the blessing of God is the force behind our liberty and our will as a people, and it is the reason we have survived as a nation. In closing, it's easy to be a patriot. You just need to love your nation.

Love America.

Chapter 29:

From God to Guns

In time, government will place even more control on gun sales within our country and limit gun manufacturers, I believe, both in overall selling of firearms and types of weapons sold. However, action taken by government will not control the minds of the millions upon millions of Americans who all ready have guns in their possession (both legally and illegally.)

Gun possession has been a legal right of American citizens since the country's founding, and it has made this country the firearm capital of the world. The Pentagon may not advertise this, but the weapons currently found in the households of the American population alone make up an army of tremendous proportion. And if you don't believe that, I am sure someone will be sending you a knucklehead hat anytime now.

A man or woman who would use a gun against another human being in a senseless act of violence is not going to be stopped by ending the future sales of guns in this country. Hell, if sick people have it in their minds to kill innocent people, what makes anyone think that the killing would not take place if a gun was not available?

Surely the lack of a gun would not stop it from happening. Perhaps they'd kill using their automobiles or kitchen knives. The bottom line is that new regulations concerning gun use or sales will never have an effect on man's desire to kill man.

The recent shooting in Arizona saddened our entire nation. Innocent people were killed by a disturbed individual. But in the aftermath, who do we blame? Some say the conservative right, led of course by talk radio (e.g., Rush and the boys). Bullshit. I have never heard Rush advocate violence in any regard. And who were the imbeciles who had the audacity to blame former Governor Palin? If that wasn't a political throw, what was it? But don't worry, Rush or Mrs. Palin. The American middle class reflects the majority of the vote in this nation, and we are not *stupid*. We also realize the gun manufacturers were not at fault. The blame for the incident and those injured and killed that day belongs squarely on the shoulders of the shooter himself. To direct blame elsewhere is a nothing more than a move on the old political game board. On the other hand, I wonder what would have happened if a licensed firearm had been in the crowd with a quick–thinking, able shooter holding its pistol grips.

Now let's talk about these crosshairs belonging to Mrs. Palin for just a moment. As a Marine of near twenty-five years, I recognize crosshairs not only as a means to target enemy but as also as a means to pinpoint objectives, whatever that objective might be. In the former governor's case, she used crosshairs on a chart to indicate items to pinpoint with a political force, not a weapon. Those lines meant nothing more than distinguishing points on a map.

I know you think I am a Republican now for sticking up for Rush and Mrs. Palin, but I am *not*. And I am not a Democrat. I just happen to think well of the two people I mentioned above, or for that matter, of any person who tries to make a difference.

Those people out there who would control the manufacturing and purchasing of guns, do you not realize that America has a greater stockpile of unlicensed, unregistered guns than any other country on Earth? This concept—even though our government wouldn't tell you—is a great and powerful factor in our national defense. We American citizens—*yes*, the United States civilian population— as we are currently armed represent the largest people's army in existence in the world today. Ask any foreign government, and they will confirm the thought. That may sound awful on one hand, but on the other hand, it's a hell of a deterrent for outsiders who might consider forcibly adjusting the borders of this great nation. If you're one of those outsiders, you may want to rethink that move. Uncle Sam will stop you—along with Uncle Jeff, Fred, Martin, Jasper, Walter, and the list goes on and on.

And speaking of borders, I remember watching *Lopez Tonight* one day and hearing the comedian joke about the United States stopping the building of the fence line along our southern-most boarder—you know, the one started to stop the flow of Mexicans illegally entering America. The joke was that the government stopped the fence construction because they came to the realization that all the Mexicans had already crossed illegally into the United States. So why build the fence?

Now I am not sure that's true, but you have to admit, it is funny. *You think?* All I have to say is if it's true, the Department of Motor Vehicles has a hell of a problem ahead with the requests for driver's licenses for that bunch. The part about this that bothers me is Mexicans are truly beautiful people. Well, maybe not so much George Lopez himself, but as a whole they truly are an attractive people and culture. Damn it, *just use the front door*. And George, you may not be the most pretty, but you are one funny guy. I love George Lopez's show. How the hell did I get on the border subject again?

Let's talk about gun control in Israel. You remember the Jews, our friends in the Middle East? You know, those same friends our government has been shying away from lately. What's up with that? Are we so worried about the goddamn Arabs? Again, back to the Jews. I mention them because I like the answer they give to gun control. It's the same answer they use for nuclear arms talk: No, we won't let you look at or diffuse our capability. Mess with us and you will see our capability (we will put it in your face). These are brave, kick-ass, honorable people. No wonder they are God's chosen people.

As for my religion, we'll continue to make denials and continue to buy our beer at liquor store drive-through windows. I do miss you, Ronald Regan. Since you left us for that better place, I want you to know more evil empires have appeared, and many sell us oil, but we still have the balls and the guns, so we're okay.

Chapter 30:

The Dollar

One percent of the world's people control 99 percent of the world's wealth; I would imagine that as a nation, America reflects that statistic as well. Did you know the Obama administration has printed more money during its tenure than any other administration ever, at any time in America's history? Actually, it's printed more than all the other administrations combined.

I believe the idea for this rash of money printing came from that famous institute born of the thirties known as the Moe, Larry, and Curly Institute for Economic Growth and Security. Did you know the average worker in China makes ten cents an hour? If you didn't know that, then you had better know this: if our government continues printing money and putting it into circulation the way it is currently doing, American workers are going to be earning dollars that are worth nearly the same as those workers in China.

What effect will the printing of additional dollars have on you? It means you may be spending twenty dollars for a loaf of bread in the future, the *near* future (exaggerated a bit). You don't even want to talk about the purchase of an automobile. Does that mean your hourly wage will increase to compensate? I don't think so. I think you're just screwed. However, what is really scary is the thought of these dollars saturating the country and the world. As the dollar continues to dwindle down in value, taxes will continue to be extracted from it hand over fist as our truly obese government continues rely more and more on that tax base. By definition, the invisible tax base is money government spends above and beyond a balanced budget. The theory is much the same as you having forty dollars in your checking account and you turning around and writing checks for two or three times that amount. Invisible tax base, my ass. It's plain foolishness.

Chapter 31:

Disturbing Facts and Tragic Americas Loss

M any factors lend themselves to America's values declining, along with a tragic loss of respect for our country's past, its government, and its moral values. The following are just a few.

Lawsuits in favor of restrictions on pledging allegiance to the American flag; no more prayer in school; congressmen and congresswomen who are not concerned with the contents of the United States Constitution; television with titles like *16 and Pregnant*; the United States giving the Panama Canal away for no good reason (and now we have to pay to use the thing); kids who wear their pants below their ass cheeks; America's gas prices driven by Arab oil; nearly two-thirds of the federal budget going to entitlements; half of American citizens living off the remaining funds; capable yet nonworking Americans living and breeding in government housing (that they may never leave); American parents afraid to give their children a swat because of child protection laws; American jobs being shuffled out of the country; Bibles being restricted from workplaces; hate groups being organized via the Internet; our government printing dollars to the point that our American dollar is said to be near (if not) at the bottom of global currency; heads of state calling our nation a second-rate power, twelfth-rate, etc., in open forum.

How do you feel about the walls now? Shall I continue?

The American penal system turned into institutions of terror brought about by the prisoners themselves; sexual predators using the Internet to seek out our children; the Social Security retirement age escalating and escalating (keep it up and perhaps they'll all be dead before the government has to pay out the cash); word from Washington that kids can't resist stealing; 30 percent of American kids not graduating high school. And the list goes on and on.

Any single point above may not seem like a significant problem, but these facts together paint a terrible picture for America's future. Worried about walls yet?

Don't be. Not yet anyway.

Chapter 32:

One Nation under God

One nation under God. How many of you out there truly believe this phrase represents the America of today? Should we have taken God and prayer out of schools? I don't think so. So why is removing prayer from school such an issue with the majority of Americans? We should have found some common ground in the ruling relating to removing God and prayer, like *to each his own* to start with. But to totally remove prayer was a callous act and against the vision of the founders of this nation.

I know to some of you think those guys were a bunch of old guys with limited vision. Well, I say you're wrong. They had great vision and even greater tenacity and strength to make it all come to fruition. But how can we average Americans argue with the high courts? After all, they always make the right choice and take the correct action. *Not.* How many of you remember the Dred Scott decision when the courts declared black people were to be looked at as property?

The fact is that courts do from time to time make bad decisions, *very bad decisions*, as they did once again by removing God and prayer from schools. The truly great part about being American is that we have rights within our Constitution that provide our people with safeguards against bad law and bad government. We can repeal bad law, and we can amend law, just as Dred Scott was overturned.

Think about it. The Declaration of Independence had it right from the get go: all men are created equal. And *our* American Constitution is very much a blueprint formed from that document. Do any of you recall a statement relating to our people having the right to continually exercise the right to amend law? We also have the right to dismantle and overthrow a corrupt government, and our forefathers gave us that right. God forbid. (Oh sorry, I wasn't supposed to say God in public. Too bad, I did it anyway.)

I truly feel that removing God from anything should have been a decision based on the will of the American people. The courts, however, based their decision on the letter of the law, and as an American I have a problem with a law that does not represent the will, mind, and hearts of the people, especially if the law distorts constitutional reasoning. I think we all felt the blow when the law took God away from our children in school. The fact is, had the question of removing God from school come up in the courts in the days of the founders, the action taken by the high court would *not* have resulted in the same decision. Why? Because the will of the people would have been represented in the decision, and it would have been aligned with a constitutional view by men that recognized God as a building block of the constitution itself

Today the will of the people is too often overlooked, as is God. I think anyone with a reasonable ability to think would agree. And what does reasonable thinking have to do with law making? Everything, my friends. Everything. Ask any attorney with a half of a brain, and he or she would say the same thing. The fact is that a law that allowed our children to pray in school could have been applied, as our forefathers would have wanted, with some simple logic. For example, if there are those who have no belief in a god, then let them not participate. As far as there being different religions, allow each student to seek his or her own way of exalting and communicating with his or her god in his or her own way. And if that process further offends the various groups, then perhaps silent prayer is the answer. But the thought of removing God altogether is just plain wrong.

I think it was President Kennedy who said something to the effect that we as a nation should ask His blessing and His help but know that here on Earth God's work must truly be our own. Faith, my friend, is apparent in every page of American history, and it needs to be in every page of our future.

Abraham Lincoln—if ever a patriot lived, it was him. His presidency toiled through a war that tore the heart out of America, and it was him and his godly beliefs that healed the nation. Lincoln had great faith in God yet no tie to a particular church. With that in mind, would anyone question his devotion to God? Of course not. America must never forget God's importance in our nation's history, just as it must never let its faith in God falter. One thing is for sure: if we let God disappear from our nation, so shall we as a nation disappear.

Chapter 33:

A Dangerous Vote

Every American has the right to vote. It's a birthright you might say. Our forefathers believed in sharing the dream. However, our forefathers never met the American population that doesn't provide and that lives off the sweat and toil of others. Those who live off the American taxpayer and contribute nothing in return should not have the right to select this country's leadership. Votes from this mass of welfare-addicted US citizens is the reason this country cannot free itself from the bounds and chains of entitlement abuse.

The fact is that the size of this group, this special-interest nightmare, grows unchallenged by proper scrutiny of the programs in which they take part, and they carry *significant* voting power. These smaller populations are always well organized and are always reaching into the taxpayers' pockets.

This group's ability to grow, combined with their ignorance at the voting booths, is of primary interest to politicians, particularly those lowlife bastards who coddle these groups. They coddle them not for what this group contributes to the wellness of our nation; instead they go after them because the government handouts they are addicted to represent easily captured votes. Certain lowlife politicians seek out this mound of American ignorance and shuffle them right into their self-serving hands, disregarding the terrible burden these people place on the stability of the nation.

Americans who live of the government and our tax dollars vote to protect that kind of lifestyle, and they will vote for any politician who promises to protect the system to which they are so addicted. In many cases, that same system that feeds and houses them. But to most of the sleazy politicians that champion such causes, they and programs they live off of are truly nothing but a way into office (or a way to keep the seat). Once in the seat, they say and do enough to keep these programs going, and they later saddle up their own agenda, most likely a self-oriented agenda at that. I may be wrong about all this, but I don't think so. What do you think?

People who live off the government and our tax dollars should not have a right to vote; the right to vote should only be reinstated when they have gained and can prove employment to a point where they too are shaken down by the Internal Revenue System.

I believe that bill would fly, and again it would have no earmarks and could be written on *one page*.

Chapter 34:

America in Your Face

Right or wrong, is it not it clear that many nations outside the United States don't particularly care for America? It's not our people they dislike; it's our government's nose in everyone's business to which they don't respond well. They don't like the will of our people butting into the will of theirs. Of course, we Americans know it's for their own good. Bullshit, and it's not the will of the American people that is to blame; it's our government's inability to mind its own business. The village idiot can see that.

Maybe our nation needs to mind its own business a little more and keep our way of life just that—our way of life—and leave the others to themselves. We don't need to interject our beliefs and will onto others to be a great nation. We already are a great nation, and in my mind we are the greatest of all nations. Think about it. We are the greatest of all nations because we are a people and a land and a country that is made up of the people from all lands. The way we attack foreign issues outside this land of ours, you would think we were the government cornerstone of world. At times we act as if we have the ability to provide the correct actions and answers to *all* the world's problems. What and/or who gives us that right? Answer: nothing and no one. We have no such right.

Reasonable-thinking people can't blame the nations around us for their negative views of America. Heck, I don't want my neighbor in my kitchen, messing with my food. America's own people see our nation at times as the global policemen, yet we stand with our cops overseas as our borders are being compromised. We need to stay in our own backyard just like we tell our kids to do, and for the exact same reason: so we can watch over and protect them.

I woke up one day to news relating to Egypt's riots in the streets and government overthrow in progress. I watched and listened to Hillary Clinton as she spoke about the situation and then later to a conversation between our president and Egypt's leader. I listened to our president give advice to this other world leader, and as I listened I couldn't help but feel the actions our president was recommending were very much needed here in our country.

Can they not see how close this nation is to an uprising provoked by similar political circumstances: civil unrest because of a faltering economy, widespread unemployment, a government exceeding its authority, government's wasteful spending, and most importantly, government movements not focused on the will of its people but instead on agendas that disrupt and discourage them?

The unrest in the Arab world is just that: unrest in the Arab world. We have too many problems within our own nation to bind ourselves to yet another world conflict, in particular a conflict in which American culture is disliked and hated. Does anyone smell oil besides me? For God's sake, we need to clean up our own country. We need to find oil on our own land, we need to search out alternative fuels, and we need to not endanger American GIs once again. And most importantly, we need to stop doing these things and getting *nothing in return.*

We gain *nothing* from this type intervention except an increase in our national debt. What do we lose? We lose American lives. On top of the bringing of these GIs home dead and wounded, we can't even protect them in burial services from asinine extremists who would disgrace them and their souls with signs that read "Thank God for dead soldiers." I don't care what that pig of a church's views are on any damn thing. They crossed the line when they decided to disrupt that GI's burial. Those bastards crossed the line. Our system of law failed our honorable dead that day. Law that acts against the will of the people is bad law and therefore needs to be adjusted. And I am not belittling our Constitution; I am talking about the will of the people, not allowing law to be misused for selfish, radical views of dissident groups

The American people want its leadership to concern itself with our nation's problems as viewed by the people. The people are the *majority*. We must stop distorting the intent of our Constitution and its law with radical applications that are destructive to the very document itself.

Our nation's government needs to return home and get back to the chore of protecting our people. Get back to loving our nation and our way of life. Get back to the work of making our nation the emblem of freedom and prosperity for the world.

Government lately has been a lot of things, but not a lot of those things are to be admired. Government is not the solution to our problems; it is the source. Ronald Regan said that, I think. Our government and its leaders—all the way up to the president himself—need to focus on cutting spending to a degree never before imagined; it needs to reduce its size; it needs to cut away the wasteland of programs that encourage those who would live endlessly off the government to continue their greedy missions; and it needs to bring America's jobs *home*, along with its military. And most importantly, it needs to stay home and out of every other nation's business.

I would like to be the president just for one day. I'd flog those bastards who protested that soldier's funeral. Disgraceful, absolutely disgraceful. I'd apply the whip myself. I most likely wouldn't be the president the next day, but hell, it would be worth it.

Chapter 35:

Too Far from the Flag Pole

I think one of the government's main flaws in correcting problems is that they never reach far enough into the problem at hand to truly understand it. In part, this failure results from highly educated people in the problem solving mode with no understanding, real vision, or life experience in the problems they intend to correct (too far away from the flag pole to raise the flag).

Face it, how many of those who have doctorate degrees live, for example, in public housing? Or for that matter, how many have lately traversed the streets of a public housing complexes or talked to residents? That's not to say these brilliant minds don't understand what it takes to manage/support operations within, but they have ever lived the life. It's like two GIs sitting in the foxhole (or as we called them in the corps, fighting holes). One GI is reading a *Stars and Stripes* newspaper and tells his buddy that according to an article, "Our government leaders are really behind us in this war." Suddenly his buddy turns and says, "They're behind us all right. *Way* behind us," meaning the government are so far behind them that it may not have the urgency, the knowledge, or even the concern to truly want the shit to end. Not to mention the fact that it is pretty safe from danger at distance, which allows it all the time in the world to solve the problem.

Solving problems often takes not just brilliant minds but people who can provide accurate description at levels of understanding no available in text books. For example, to solve public housing problems, speak to those who have managed it, maintained it, or lived in it for decades. The picture will be much clearer, and they would have quality facts and information. That's when good, sound discussion to determine an effective solution can take place and problems can be solved.

Chapter 36:

Politically Driven Objectives

Politically driven objectives nearly always abandon the people's will. And they are always party driven. A political objective today does not bring to mind political leadership working in unison to solve problems. Instead, it sadly brings thoughts of opposing political parties squabbling on one hand while screwing over the nation's people with the other.

Self- or party interest seems to be the mark of America's political parties today. Shouldn't the interest and well-being of America and its people be the underlying interest of all the political battling? Of course it should! Many Americans today believe political parties should be removed entirely from the process of choosing our government leaders. Instead of gathering perspective candidates from those who represent or conform to a party and/or a particular party's agendas, the choice of men and women in leadership should perhaps be selected without party affiliation. Selection would be based entirely on a person's integrity, drive, motivation to serve, and sincere love of this nation.

Imagine leadership elected strictly on the basis of who will honestly represent America and its citizens, who has total concern for our nation's well-being and mindfulness for the people's will in all matters, and who while doing so will always embrace our nation's values, our Constitution, our heritage, and the glory of America's future. We would be able to choose only those who will represent us, not with selfish self-interests but instead in a way that demonstrates loyalty to the nation, not to a party or a special interest.

I think Mr. Rick Perry hit the nail square on the head when he said the American people are tired of political correctness. What the people want is to tackle the real problems. (He may not have said it exactly like I wrote it, but my words are in the ballpark, God bless him.) Lastly, President Lincoln said—and I repeat—"A house divided cannot stand." Our current US House and Senate can't make a goddamn thing happen for that very reason (division of the political parties).

Chapter 37:

Conservative or Liberal

Conservative or liberal? That is the question. What is America's next president going to look like from that perspective? And who will decide? Liberal or conservative, extreme views can be frightening. However, I believe most working-class Americans are "right-handed." I do realize each American can go extremely left or right on any given subject; however, most middle-class Americans file behind the conservative column. Why? Because we were born of conservative people. Face it, guys, the founders of this nation were not extreme left-punchers; there was no ACLU on board when they tossed the tea into the harbor.

Think about it. Can you imagine legislation crossing the desks of people like Washington, Jefferson, or Adams concerning topics like don't ask, don't tell or the removal of God from classrooms or the removal of prayer itself? How about abortion demands or continued extensions of unemployment insurance? Could you imagine the looks on these guys' faces? Well, I have news for many of you out there: most Americans today have the same looks on their faces.

The question remains, how will the Republican presidential candidate be chosen? Will this man or women be recognized by his or her performance in the debates or by his or her true character and true potential and worth to the nation? I think *not*.

I truly believe that the candidates that best represent the Republican Party and the Tea Party will be strategically torn apart by a liberal press to a point where the best of the group will fall before the primaries, victims to wounds from character assassination unduly given to them along the road to the presidency. Why would the liberal press kill the good guys and gals? Because they know these people could bring home the bacon, and once these people are out of the way, the Republican or Tea Party selection would be like sending in the second string to win the game. And that would ultimately mean that the candidate chosen to defeat the Democratic president currently in office would be selected from the weakest of the group, who in the end will prove less of a challenge to defeat the incumbent president.

I believe the things I write; I am an independent voter whose vote is for the most part conservative. Therefore I say to you, be careful with your vote. Don't be fooled by the press picking on a particular shortfall of the guy or gal you have been liking all along. He or she is most likely the best one for the job. If not, the press wouldn't be trying to kill him or her. This of course is my opinion about the workings of a liberal press. Now, I am not telling you to turn on Rush, Hannity, Laura, or Rodney, but if you find yourself lost along the way, do so. Personally, I am partial to their conservative views.

We know liberals and conservatives basically march to the tune of different drums; however, the commonality they both inherit as Americans is the right to voice their opinions. Our forefathers gave this country that special right. I get to write this book and express my thoughts without fear of reprisal, and a liberal press gets to voice its ideas because of it.

God bless America.

Chapter 38:

The President's Vacation

I am tired of the president getting beat up for taking too many vacations or eating hamburgers on the side. It makes me laugh that the same people who say this man takes far too many vacations are the same ones who say he's not worth a damn. Well hell, if he's not worth a damn, then I would think you'd be happy when he's out of pocket on vacation, lazing around on some beach in Hawaii, eating a snow cone.

After all, how much damage to the country can a president do in that status? And how much damage to him is eating a snow cone? None. Heck, our president looks pretty healthy to me. All kidding aside, I couldn't care less how many vacations my president takes or how many snow cones he eats, particularly if he or she can do the job in between outings and eating. And as a former Marine with a presidential support clearance, I can say in all honesty from the very little time spent I spent near a US president, I never saw him on vacation even when he was on vacation.

Presidents of this nation work hard, and the job never leaves them. The job is constantly in their faces, 24-7. I wouldn't want the job. Well, maybe I'd like it for a day or two just to kick some ass, clear out the entitlement bandits, take the Arab's oil away from them, pass a bill to take care of our elderly and slow down illegal immigrant flow through our borders, and clean out the prisons. Heck, I might need four or five days. Oh yes, and let's not forget, bring the jobs and GIs home and the most important objective for this American president: "get America working again." No, thinking out loud, I may need six or seven days and a few rounds of ammunition. And lastly and most importantly, as an afterthought I'd need to get rid of the ACLU, along with ACORN and a few other radical, destructive whiner-based organizations. Of course, this is purely my view. Bullshit. Everybody I know can't stand the ACLU. Hell, anybody who works can't stand them.

Now after all this has been said, do any of you think the president really ever truly has a rest while in office? I don't. If you think so, I think one of your friends may be mailing you your own personal knucklehead hat very soon. Let's end this by saying let's hope the work our president ties himself down to is constructive work and work that is warranted by his office. This, friend, is the question. And this is the question that has been giving some folks problems lately.

By the way, how are the walls looking to you at this point?

Chapter 39:

Debt Ceiling

I am told the debt ceiling will soon no longer be a problem. As a young man, I had a thirty-three-inch waist. It was rather ideal for my body structure. That waist size stayed with me for a good part of my twenty-five years as a United States Marine. The Marine corps placed controls on how fat I could get, and I knew if I was to remain a Marine I would have to stay fit, eat right, and exercise daily to maintain that ideal weight and size.

Upon retirement, my waist quickly grew to thirty-four inches, which was still well within Marine corps standards, and I honestly felt great. So what the hell? However, within five years of retirement, that measurement went up to thirty-five and then thirty-sex inches. My waist grew pretty much for the same reason our national debt grows: lack of control and lack of proper exercise.

When it comes to weight, the lack of exercise, combined with lack of control in eating habits, causes weight gain. In the government's case, lack of control in not only the amount of spending but also in exercising good spending sense and neglecting to see the cumulative damage is the cause of debt gain. I feel like a fat pig these days with a thirty-six-inch waist. I imagine our government should feel about the size of a planet.

I truly can't understand it. Is it all just not balancing income against expenses? How can the United States government justify spending twice the income it gains from taxation? Is our government just not aware of the problem? Does it not have the skills to balance the books? When we the working classes write checks beyond the balance of our checkbooks, is it not the same thing as the government writing checks it doesn't have the money to fulfill? Sure it is. So what the hell is the problem?

They say the new health care bill will add an additional one and a half trillion more to the deficit. My God, is that possible? And if it is true, the every American needs to pick up his or her Senate and House member who is voting to keep it going, take them for a ride, and toss them into Boston Harbor in the same place our forefathers tossed the damn tea.

You may think this is silly of me, but I truly don't feel any Senate or House member can truly fathom what a trillion of dollars really is all about. Can you? Hell no, you can't. I believe our government leadership is not overwhelmed by these horrific dollar amounts of waste because our leaders do not have the ability to comprehend what amounts of money of this magnitude truly represent. And it is with the lack of such reasoning that these knucklehead leaders of ours make the bad decisions concerning cuts in governments spending and elevating the debt ceiling.

What needs to happen is that we need to put them all in the middle of the new Dallas football stadium playing field and fill it with a trillion dollars and make sure these leaders of ours are beneath the falling bills. (And if we don't have a trillion dollars available, just ask the current administration to print some more. I understand they have a real handle on printing money these days). After we drop a trillion of dollars on them, I guarantee the ones who survive under the weight of all that money will at that point have an understanding of the magnitude of the debt ceiling problem. And I bet capping and cutting would become very important after that.

Cumulative neglect compounded with cumulative ignorance is the problem in a nutshell. Think about it:

1. Our massive debt is *seven* times our annual tax income.
2. Almost half the government's annual spending is borrowed, which significantly adds to our deficit each year.
3. We borrow from foreign investors to help fund government's debt. How crazy is that? Who in their right mind would want the job as president knowing these things?

I listen to our president speak of not overspending in the future, which is good, but I am not sure that kind of thinking solves the problem. I believe we have to do much more than not overspend within the framework of the existing budget. We must reverse spending. We must slim down the existing budget. We must cut, cut, and cut even more. We must underspend. We must cut away at the waste and the fat.

I did not hear words relating to capping spending either. I believe Martin Luther King Jr. said, "The time is always right to do the right thing." And the right thing to do with federal spending is not just about capping it. No, instead federal spending must be radically reduced. Reducing the size of America's government sounds like a great place to start. First cut away and/or limit the useless extremities, the programs that give away taxpayer dollars and return nothing. Face it, our government is so large at this point, I guarantee our forefathers would not recognize it.

It has been said that many of the first gatherings of our government took place in taverns. Not today, baby. There's no beer joint big enough to unleash today's government in it—a government with a waist size in the trillions. All joking aside, *we* must insist our leaders refrain from continual overspending. The American people could help in this capping and cutting. The problem is that the American people are so out of touch with federal spending, how could they possibly provide input?

Three cheers for Arkansas; my state and its government leadership are about to get the people involved, and more importantly, they are about to lay out the budget so all the state's residents can see and understand it. Lieutenant Governor Darr has put forth the vision that the Arkansas budget will in the future be totally transparent for all to read and understand. It is to be written, as I understand it at this point, in a comprehensive and easy language that guys like me who aren't too smart can read. And hopefully after viewing the state expenditures, those guys will make intelligent decisions as voters when it comes to what the state's government is spending money on. God Bless, Arkansas. And you all thought we were just pretty and natural. The fact is that we are pretty *smart* and natural.

I have to admit, our governor stands fast on keeping the old budget in line and balanced. Yep, we have a Democrat for a governor (Mike Beebe) and a Republican for a lieutenant governor (Mark Darr), both of whom I greatly respect. In this particular case, the two of them bring out the best in the political parties and bipartisan work effort. Their justification for doing so, I say, is the good of the people they represent. As for me, I am not a party boy, but I would vote for both of them again.

Debt ceiling talk without mentioning the reduction or removal of several of the unearned entitlements is talk without substance. We are just dancing around the issue at hand, again tossing that hot potato. We as a nation spend too much on taking care of people who should be taking care of themselves. That is the bottom line in controlling the debt in America. The *bottom line.*

Have you ever asked yourself why China can sell about anything it makes (except toothpaste—that shit will kill you) in the United States, with no tax requirement, while on the other hand America can't sell jack in China? America, start taxing the shit out of the little yellow fellows and anyone else bringing products into our nation. Guess what? Jobs will rain across the country when that happens. American government, you haven't figured that out? I have to ask, what kind of hold does China have on us?

Hell, we can shovel our US coal out to them by the boatloads, but we can't mine it for ourselves. What's up with that? I smell some tree-hugging idiot behind this asinine situation. I wish I could be the president just for one day. I would spend every minute of the day firing the dumb son of britches every minute of that day. (I'm trying to watch my language. You never can tell where Mother is with that bar of soap.) And all you pantywaist motor scooters out there, don't judge me. Remember Mathew 7:1.

In closing, I want to say that President Obama's wife, Michelle, is a beautiful and caring person. I don't care what these knuckleheads say about her. She is exactly how I just described, and her campaign designed around reducing obesity in American youth is again a wonderful idea, a truly great cause. But perhaps it can be modified to a degree and expanded into removing the fat from our obese government and its incredible spending habits. What do you think?

A government that is too large and wasteful can't be responsive to the needs of a nation. It's just too fat and too lost (again, very much the picture of a severely obese person).

As for you, first lady, God bless you.

Chapter 40:

The Problem in a Nutshell

The wasteland. The United States government. How did it get so out of control? Have you ever asked yourself what the common denominator is? What in today's United States government caused the growth and the government's seemingly endless attraction in exercising control over a list of items that are in no way aligned with its framework? And how did this powerful world-leading nation of ours diminish in status so overwhelmingly quickly?

In my opinion, the common negative factor in every questionable activity within this nation festers around a common disregard of the voice and will of the American people and the current government's ridiculous and seemingly never-ending allegiance to the powers of special interest groups.

The volume of special interest activity in which our government involves itself is unprecedented, especially in the waste and burden that comes with every misused American dollar. Face it: this thought in a nutshell is the major cause of this country's collapsing economy. The irony of it all is that the amount of people represented by special interest groups/activity in no way justifies the overwhelming spending used to appease them. Yes, this little giant has an appetite one hundred times its size.

For example, those on food stamps in this nation represent approximately 43.5 million people, which equates to about 15 percent of the overall population. As a portion of the population, this is a relatively small group; however, as a funding requirement, it represents a powerful chunk of the federal spending budget, with no return attached. And food stamps are just one of hundreds upon hundreds of money-gutting expenses in the world of special interests. Trust me, it is the no-return–attached entitlements that are the main menace to the budgets and the primary reason people who receive them continue to use them day after day, year after year, generation after generation.

If you don't believe that, then go on being stupid. To really get an idea how powerful of a burden these special interest groups put on state and federal budgets and how they contribute to debt ceiling increases, look at California as an example. This particular state's illegal immigrant population on a yearly basis costs the state government about twenty billion dollars. That's a lot of money, right? Now look at California's current budget deficit, which is upward of twenty five billion dollars.

Now what if this population of illegal immigrants was removed? What would it do for the California deficit? Well, what it would do is make it nearly manageable. Think about it. This special interest alone—this population of illegal immigrants by itself— pretty much capsized California's budget in one year, nearly twenty billion dollars worth. It kind of makes it easy to understand how the federal government feeding so many different special interests has contributed trillions upon trillions to the disastrous buildup of the federal deficit.

It's not just the deficit that makes me mad. It's the fact that these special interest groups have cost the middle class over a third of their income in taxes (in reality, closer to half). They've also caused a tremendous decline in economic growth in our land, and sadly I see no end unless we start talking about severe cuts in federal spending. But no, instead we'd rather discuss driver's licenses for illegal immigrants in presidential debates. America, it is time to say enough is enough. We cannot and will not vote into office any person who cannot see the real problems that plague America as a nation.

Reform, reduce, and remove entitlement programs. The American government is out of control, not as the result of the needs of the many but instead for the needs of the few—the greedy and the lazy. The American government is comparable to an obese person whose diet consists of ingesting food with total disregard to the person's body framework or health requirements. And just as this obese person's organs and body parts begin to fail him or her because of this tremendous weight gain, so have the government's parts and extremities begun to fail. The government's appetite for special interests must be controlled and curbed if we are to survive as a nation, and its exercise of the will of the people must increase. It's very simple.

Chapter 41:

The Final Chapter

Our government was designed to support the Constitution and the American way of life described within it; it is supposed to protect our country's freedoms and democracy. Yet lately its powers have broadened into diverse and unhealthy handling of things far from the Constitution's original intent. Sadly, the responsibilities it has saddled itself with are becoming a burden not only to itself but to the people it serves.

Our country's beauty lies in the diversity of its people—everything from skin color to the beautiful minds that reflect heritages from all parts of the globe. The people of this wonderful nation, however, are losing faith in government and its ability to conduct business. Government powers have entered into a gamut of controversial arenas, where every turn seems to place additional financial burden on its people (primarily the middle-class segment of the nation).

The people are outraged at the lack of control placed on government spending and the seeming inability of our leaders to recognize the harm created by overspending. Our people are tired of a tremendous amount of the population of Americans who live off the rest of us. We worry about our dreams disappearing, all at the hand of weak, incompetent, selfish, undisciplined (and some corrupt) legislators. During the Lincoln-Douglas debates, Lincoln made a statement something to the effect that a house divided against itself cannot stand. I believe that statement was as true then as it is now and as spoken in the good book (Matthew 12:25).

Lincoln also expressed disagreement with the practice of "You work and toil and earn bread, and I will eat it." Of course then Lincoln's words were aimed at the injustice slavery posed in our nation at the time, but today's middle class can apply those same words to their plight. Yes, the middle class is outright tired of feeding the lazy and housing the poor, the poor who refuse to work. We are tired of our government's approach to helping the less fortunate (those who desire to live off the government and who have become addicted over several generations to living off it), doing so at the expense of working men and women. We are tired of a government that helps them and expects nothing in return, giving it all away at the expense of the middle class (or should I say at the expense of the working class) of the United States.

The process as a whole is asinine; the imbalance it creates allows the rich to get richer, the poor to be driven through life with no accountability, and working American citizens to foot the bill for the entirety as they toil through life, working hard while watching their dreams slip away. Government is being manipulated by lobbyists that sell everything from the lazy poor to insurance and big business (like pharmaceutical companies and automobile manufacturers and companies that build their products out and away from the American workforce and then turn around and sell them to middle-class Americans at exorbitant prices). This all must *end*.

In closing, you might say: I am America's average Joe (not to be mistaken for that plumber fellow). I love America and the American way of life. I spent the youth of my life and much of my manhood in the uniform of a United States Marine. I served my country with pride in peace and in war. I never did anything brave or heroic. I, like millions before me, followed orders and went where I was told without question, honoring my country as best I could along the way. I love this nation, its leaders, and its people most of all. The fact that America is filled with a rainbow of races, religions, and immigrants from every corner of the Earth makes this country truly special. America is truly a wonderful nation. I say that as a man who has been to several countries around the world and has always come home realizing how wonderful America truly is.

It is my wish as an American that we as a people always put our self-interests, our skin colors, our religious beliefs, and our lands of origin to work in an effort to make the title of American citizen one of, if not *the*, ranking priorities in our lives.

Together, we are the people of the greatest nation ever created on this Earth.

God bless America.

The American Creed

I believe in the United States of America as a government of the people, by the people, for the people; whose just powers are derived from the consent of the governed; a democracy in a republic; a sovereign Nation of many sovereign States; a perfect union, one and inseparable; established upon those principles of freedom, equality, justice, and humanity for which American patriots sacrificed their lives and fortunes.

I therefore believe it is my duty to my country to love it, support its Constitution, to obey its laws, to respect its flag, and to defend it against all enemies.

—William Tyler Page, adopted by the United States House of Representatives on April 3, 1918

This is a special note to all of you chosen by the people of America to serve as leaders of this great country: You would do well to take this creed to heart and memory. You are the voice of the governed. You serve at the discretion of the people you represent. Do not turn a deaf ear to your constituents. Remember, you represent the heart, will, and minds of those who elected you—a government of the people for the people.

It is time, and as Dr. Martin Luther King Jr. said, "It's always the right time to do the right thing." Do not belittle those you represent by altering our direction to your desires; instead, proudly carry our torch, particularly if you enjoy the prestigious title and seat to which you have been so graciously elected, because without our support, you won't be sitting in it for very much longer. We *will* vote your butts right out.

As for America's walls, they are standing strong and with honor, as always.

God bless America.

About the Author

Tom Forbes, retired US Marine, a man who does not earn a living through his writings, if you read this book you may understand why. Tom served his nation during peace and war for approximately twenty-five years of his youth; never performed an act of bravery or heroism, just served honorably as did thousands of Marines before him. He, however, writes not as a former Marine, but instead as a concerned average American citizen who is tired of a government that seems to turn a deaf ear to the voices of the working middle-class of this nation (other wise know as this Nations Tax payers). Tom is no longer an active duty Marine he is however on a mission. A mission to unit fellow working class Americans to speak out and fight for the well being of themselves and as well the Nation itself. As an author Tom does not expect all who read this book to rally around his every word. However, in the many chapters within he is sure much of the words will sound reasonable to the reader. It is his hope that his voice and reasoning within the pages will inspire others to speak out and be heard. Tom is not Mr. Smith who goes to Washington, but he would vote for anyone who resembled the man.

American Knucklehead Hat and T-Shirt

To order: an American Knucklehead Hat or T-shirt for one of your *Stupid friends*, send your request to P.O. Box 1311 Camden AR 71711-2311

The total cost, including shipping and handling, is $25.00 per hat (one to a customery). Tee Shirts $ 22 dollars cost, including shipping and handling (one to a customer). To have the hat / shirt autographed by yours truly, there is an additional $2 charge. Checks, Cash, or Money orders, will be accepted. (Checks must clear prior to order being filled).

A tea shirt added to a hat order total cost $ 37.00 (includes Payment/s shipping and hanldling for both items.

Again one of each to a customery

Or dial 1-367-386-2277 (for dumb ass) just kidding, no such number. Clearly Request In writing:

Request: 1 American Knucklehead Hat   / Total cost $ 25.00
Request 1 American Knucklehead Tea shirt (Large)   / Total cost $22.00
Request Both 1 American Knucklehead Hat & 1 Teas shit / Total cost $37.00

All Tea shirt request must in clued Size Small, Medium, Large or Extra large.

Note: EBT cards Not Excepted Not Now, not ever......